Day Pass
From The Asylum

This volume is dedicated, not only to those I succeeded because of, but also the ones I succeeded in spite of... my teachers, my professors and my family...*they* know who *they* are !

I owe much of my inspirations to the brave souls who have traveled the dark paths through depression and mental illness and have, somehow, come out on the other side of the light. Also, to the doctors, the nurses and the therapists who have dedicated their lives to this cause, who have held our hands along the way and set us free on the other side.

Meryl C. Taylor

(MEL)

Signature
HEALTH

When you need help now.

August 18, 2011

To Whom It May Concern,

I would like to introduce Meryl Taylor as a colleague and personal friend. She has been blessed with a unique ability to capture human experiences by the pen in her poetry. Meryl has been writing wonderful poems from an early age and has been very successful in her more recent efforts of compiling a trilogy of hundreds of her finest works. Meryl has the unique ability to capture human experience in few, but carefully chosen words. She has the gift of the great romantic poets and has developed a unique poetic style, which has been perfected much like the limerick or the sonnet. It has been a privilege and a pleasure to read all of her works in her three-book trilogy. It has been very exciting to watch her efforts be shared by thousands as her books are now available in bookstores. Very few can frame a moment in time with such detail and wit, cloaked in rhyme by Meryl Taylor.

Without reservation, I would give my highest recommendation on behalf of Meryl Taylor as she will continue to succeed in her efforts to capture these times in her rhymes. If I may be of any further service to Meryl, please feel free to notify me at Signature Health in Ashtabula, Ohio.

Respectfully,

Todd J. Gates D.O.

Todd Gates, DO
TG:pf/jf ~ 62797

Day Pass From The Asylum

Meryl Taylor

To order additional copies of this book, contact:
Xlibris Corporation
1-888-795-4274
www.Xlibris.com
Orders@Xlibris.com
89646

Contents

THE GOOD SHEPHERD

The good shepherd
He leadeth me into implausible trust.
I am to follow,
taking goodness for granted.
The good shepherd
discovers my lack,
promising to fulfill my needs,
requiring my submission.
The good shepherd
vows to save my soul.
I need only believe everything,
no matter how fantastical.
The good shepherd
insures more than He can deliver
if I do all required of me,
even if it's painful.
The good shepherd
He leadeth me over my head
to mountains too vast to climb
to air too rarified to breathe.
The good shepherd
only wants what is best for me,
to follow blindly
into the path of my distruction.

I SEE

I see such rage in my older children,
a volatile, subcutaneous layer
of anger and pain.
I see such loss of innocense,
a cavernous void of hurt,
a lack of feeling and conscience.
I see such a dirth of joy,
a cacaphonous shriek,
a roaring wave of hatred.
I see my lack too evident,
magnified ten fold in their faces;
a dark, foreboding perception of life.
I see my failures on their psyches,
a betrayal of attitude,
an ignorance of what is required.

LITTLE BOY, LITTLE BOY

Little boy, little boy,
where have you gone?
To the land of dragons,
of our fiery spawn?
Little boy, little boy
where have you gone?
To dark, sweaty caverns
to hide from the dawn?
Little boy, little boy,
what have you seen?
Monsters? Demons?
to inhabit your dreams?
Little boy, little boy,
what do you say?
Who wants all the answers
to show you the way?
Little boy, little boy,
when will you forgive
shortcomings and failings
before you can live?
Little boy, little boy,
when will you see
that life's what you make it?
Don't fall to a knee.
Little boy, little boy,
when will you be a man
who holds his head higher
to see all that he can?

THERE ONCE WAS A MAN

There once was a man
who gave a ring for my finger
to keep me in bondage
concede his demands.
There once was a man
who believed we should marry
to curtail independence
or ideas that vary.
There once was a man
who would create me a wife
to cleave only to him
for the rest of my life.
There once was a man
who made every rule,
who tried to convince me
that I was a fool.
There once was a man
who never would dance,
who tried to lure me
into dire circumstance.
There once was a man
who gave me a child,
set me free, gave new life
and at last was reconciled.

I BEQUEATHE

I bequeathe to the world
my love of all life;
my joy as a mother,
my bliss as a wife.
I bequeathe to my children
my one sacrfice,
the give and the take
that will have to suffice.
I bequeathe to my husband
my thoughts and emotion
to love him forever with utter devotion.
I bequeathe to my soul
my stark revelation
to judge no one person
in any relation.
I bequeathe to myself
my honest contrition
to maintain every essence
in humble ambition.
I bequeathe to the world,
at heavens request,
my sincere understanding
of what I do best.
I bequeathe to the people
I encounter each day
to be kind, to be friendly
in every way.
I bequeathe to the heavens
my sincere appreciation
to all things cerebral,
for all things in creation.
I bequeathe to the masses
what my spirit commends
to be just and be grateful
as my heart recommends.

MY PATH

My path has been much longer
than was planned for in my past.
My steps have been determined
yet I do not travel fast.
My path has been a circuit
with many turns and curves
that led to many problems
my carelessness deserves.
My path is steep for climbing,
vast horizons break ahead.
I could have taken any road
yet I chose rough ones instead.
My paths traverse a great abyss
precedes the desert floor
where I endured lifes problems
a phoenix needing more.
My path leads back to places
I have always called my home,
where I may rest again one day,
when I need no longer roam.
My path beckins follow me
to vistas far above
where I will know contentment,
where naught is known but love.

WE POETS

We poets know not of numbers,
save for meter, rhyme.
The numerals upon a clock
regarding worldly time.
We poets care not for science,
save elements of fire
to light the world with passions
borne of young desire.
We poets know no direction
while searching for our voices,
sparking words of longing, words of life
while every sphere rejoices.
We poets know not of bondage
the pragmatist must feel.
We appreciate abstract forms
as relevent and real.
We poets render words with craft
blending shape and depth and love
as whispers, shout from mountain tops
to everything above.

ALWAYS QUESTION "WHY?"

Think for yourself.
Don't be a fool
for anyone who deighns to rule.
Always question "Why?"
Think for yourself.
Own your own soul.
Allow no man to seize control.
Always question "Why?"
Think for yourself.
Don't take a chance
on images poised to entrance.
Always question "Why?"
Think for yourself.
Stand firm, run fast.
Struggle for freedom to the last.
Always question "Why?"
Think for yourself.
You will not fail
to succed against some dark travail.
Always question "Why?"
Think for yourself.
You'll be the one
remaining sure when day is done.
Always question "Why?"
Think for yourself.
Don't heed the chatter.
It's your ideas that truly matter.
Always question "Why?"

NOW I KNOW MYSELF

Once, long ago, I was afraid
of promises broken, debts unpaid;
of all foundations hastily laid.
Now, I know myself.
Once, long ago, I always questioned "Why?"
Instead of smiles, I chose to cry
for every tempest crashing by.
Now, I know myself.
Once, long ago, I'd never ask,
allow myself to shine, to bask.
No longer timid, behind a mask,
Now, I know myself.
Once, long ago, I would not fight
for any cause I knew was right.
I trembled every day from fright.
Now, I know myself.
Once, long ago, I could not allow
myself to laugh, to livebut, now,
I have finally learned just how.
Now, I know myself.

THE PRINCESS WON'T GROW UP

The queen of drama plays the part
meant to wound my aching heart.
The curtain's raised, the act will start.
The princess won't grow up.
The scene is set upon the stage
for every audience to engage
the script imprinted on the page.
The princess won't grow up.
She has rehearsed her speech with zeal
in case her sullied truths reveal
the darkest secrets she would conceal.
The princess won't grow up.
This vexing woman she's become-
false to most, unkind to some-
the lies bandied about are mum.
the princess won't grow up.
The curtain falls, the stage is bare.
Lights, applause cannot compare
with revelations garnered there.
the princess won't grow up.
She gleans approval from it all.
the stage lights dim, the curtains fall.
Exit, stage left, into the hall.
The princess won't grow up.
The Queen of drama plays the part
that breaks and binds this mothers heart.
She bids teh audience, "Depart"
The princess won't grow up.

MY UNTIDY LIFE

I have experienced many things
in my untidy life.
I have loved well but not always wisely.
My life has been full of color
of music and vibration,
from the depths of sorrow,
I have risen, a phoenix, from my own ashes.
I recoil from the small-minded strictures,
choking me, squeezing the life, the breath from my soul.
My intergrity has survived deceit,
broken promises of the well-meaning
who would rather look good than be good.
I have survived so many things
in my untidy life.
Earthly days of happy luck,
days of abusive plenty.
Love and loss revolves around me,
scattering the remnants of my untidy life.

YOU KNOW ME

You know me
in the deepest, darkest places
when I'm void of all the graces,
when I'm mired in my disgraces,
you know me
through my path of other lovers
when patience soon recovers
from the ghost the subtly hovers
you know me
in the depths of my despair
I know you are always there
with love, support and grace to share
you know me
when the world denies my choices,
when our agony rejoices
the power of love anoints us
you know me
through all my darkest days
you clear the dust to send suns rays
while finding truth in fresh delays
You know me.

OH, WOMEN

Oh, women,
we are put upon,
dragged down by reverance.
We are held to a standard,
held in dire esteem for some part
of giving life.
Oh, women,
we are put upon,
when we become a wife,
our selves, our souls as individuals
are choked, strangled, murderd by high regard.
Oh, women,
we are put upon
we do not give life alone,
not of consequence in the making of decisions,
of conferring blessings.
Oh, women,
we are put upon
to change diapers, wipe noses
with the foot of our men on our necks,
to cook, to clean, to labor.
Oh, women,
we are put upon.

OH, MOMMY

Oh, mommy
There are questions we must ask.
I fear we must take you to task
now that you are gone.
Oh, mommy
What made you choose a life,
leaving youth to be a wife
with so much of your life left undone?
Oh, mommy,
How could you have a child,
thus being somehow reconciled
never to return once you'd begun.
Oh, mommy,
time cannot erase
each tear-stained little face
that watched wondering as you moved on.
Oh, mommy,
I cannot express
an anger tempered tenderness
at battles fought yet never won.
Oh, mommy,
If you had only understood
we thought if we'd been good
you never would have thought to run.
Oh, mommy,
If you had ever known,
your creations, each your own
were spawned by all the lies you'd spun.
Oh, mommy,
we must all endure
without ever knowing quite for sure
if you ever loved us, to the one.

Oh, mommy,
as your soul's at last departed,
to leave us damaged, broken hearted
to whither in your unrequited sun.
Oh, mommy,
We were never quite so sure
if loss was what loved ones must endure
before much awaited answers finally come.
Oh, mommy,
Our pains, our losses, regrets have passed.
Now, morsels offered up to us must last.
the chorus quieted with many songs unsung.

SOME PEOPLE

Some people compete in marathons
while running from the past,
their deeds, their reputations
unsupported, never last.
Some people race toward excellence
to never be achieved,
all hopes, dreams and aspirations
to come true for us must be believed.
Some people hurry through their days
as if living caused delays
only to find thier position stuck forever in one place.
Some people never make a move
to travel toward their deepest dreams
to never catch the very stitch
to mend lifes straining seams.
Some people simply mark their time
secure in trusted ways,
they've wandered through each phase of life
mired as time assays.
Some people never make the stretch
while planning their escape
to run a little faster,
win the race and break on through the tape.

OPPORTUNITY

I walk the chilled streets, collar turned up against the night,
one sure step following another.
Sidewalks are bare, the snow long swept away,
pavement with a sheen of frost.
My breath goes before me,
a wisp of vapor in the wind-harbinger of weather coming.
I jam my gloveless hands deep into my empty pockets
and I smile at opportunity.
A full pocket stays the same, bulging with contents,
jangling with coin.
Only empty pockets have room for better things inside.
Bigger, brighter things to line my pockets-
things to share, to give away until they are ready to fill again.

BUTTERCUP

Buttercup sits across fom me
the picture of innocense.
Beneath this cat is evidence
he's had quite an evening.

The Christams tree is on its side
and there amid the litter
is Buttercup, my little cat,
caught up amid the littler

He lifts his head to look my way.
He yawns as if he's bored with us.
He stretches out to rest again,
oblivious to the fuss.
He's quite a cat
flexing his great paws.
(If there is any trouble here
he is surely not the cause.)
Don't believe his cool demeanor.
He can be very bold.
I can't wait to see what he does
when he's two years old.

MY HELPER

I have a little helper
as I tie the Christmas bows
who has the crinkle ribbon
wrapped up in his toes.
To my helper, say God Bless!
he sure knows how to make a mess.
he wears enough
of Christmas stuff
to be a decoration.
My Helper never gets too tired
to make a mess for us,
unwind a spool
is now the rule.
He will just ignore us.
Curiously, my sweet cat,
rests amid the paper where he sat.
He's tired out
there is no doubt
from his Christmas caper.

CATHERINE

Catherine, off the streets today,
safely tucked away,
protected from herself.
She bristles,
she fights,
she's crude.
A hunger so deep eats at her.
She mixes all her food together.
To me, it looks like garbage.
Still, she two-fists food into her maw,
talking to herself.
After meals she searches
the trays for half-eaten tidbits,
cast-off morsels of other patients.
Scooping remnants of someone elses meals
with her fingers,
she is a sad sight.
So young, so troubled, so lost . . .
Catherine, off the streets for today.

THE GREATEST GIFT

The greatest gift we have to give
comes straight from the heart.
It doesn't need a box or bow
for the act to start.
A sincere thought
for someone else
we've met along the way
that lifts sad spirits
and brighten up their day.
It doesn't have to cost alot
to be a gift, that's true.
Just loves own expression
that goes from me to you.
The biggest gift we give
becomes a paradox.
It's love and all it touches
and it never needs a box.
Love comes in every shape and size-
never too large or small
wrapped up in sentimentality,
a given love fits all.

MY GIFT TO YOU

Here's my gift.
It is for you.
It's what I have selected
to tell you what you mean to me
so you won't feel neglected.
It's wrapped in special paper
and tied up in a bow
to let you know I love you more
than you will ever know.
Each day has been a treasure;
each week, each month, each year;
a cache of jewels so rare
that I hold so dear.
To see you every morning.
To see you every night
reminds me of the reasons
we so seldom fight.
Your eyes, your smile, your guiless ways
disarming as they are
make me glad I found you
and we are who we are.

OH, CHRISTMAS TREE

Oh, Christmas tree, oh, Christmas tree
how bare now are your branches.
The cats have all discoverd you
and knocked off a ball or two.
Oh, Christmas tree, oh, Christmas tree,
how bare now are your branches.
The tinsel is all on the floor.
The angel rests beside the door.
Oh, Christmas tree, oh, Christmas tree
How bare now are your branches.
The tabby lays amid the mess
of several presents, more or less.
Oh, Christmas tree, oh Christmas tree.
How bare now are your branches.
The little tom sits on a limb.
There's nothing now to persuade him
that he should leave the Christmas tree
while it still has some branches.

FROM METRO IV

You have given me so much
a box could never hold;
no paper could wrap,
no ribbon bind.
It filled a void so long ago
so vast, a world so cold,
because you were so kind.

CHRISTMAS BLOWS

It happened to me again this year,
I swear by Rudolphs nose
I'm becoming Mrs. Scrooge.
I tell you, Christmas blows!

I wrapped all the presents bought
but I guess it shows
I'm giving up the Christmas ghost.
I tell you Christmas blows!

Each person got s present.
I'm giving, everybody knows.
Naught for me beneath the tree.
I tell you christmas blows!

I made cookies, bought the ham,
that's always how it goes.
Tonight I fed the multitudes.
I tell you Christmas blows!

When Christmas season comes next year
I'm going to thumb my nose
at every Merry Cristmas wish.
I tell you, Christmas blows!

AWAKEN, NOW

Awaken, now, from threadbare dreams,
from nights of fitful sleep.
Illusion is not all it seems
in secrets that you keep.
Awaken, now, to morning light.
Another night you've slept
safely from the evenings plight
    and all the tears you've wept.
Awaken, now, to realities glare
and all that we perceive
cast away now without a care
things we do not dare believe.
Awaken, now, the day is new.
What's possible is great.
Look ahead to what's in veiw
before it is too late.

THE CHRISTMAS MYTH

Christmas is past.
People cling to their threadbare religion-
the Holy family, the virgin birth, we three kings . . .
Reason has run out.
Romantic notions prevail;
Santa and the Baby Jesus; Rudolph and Frosty the Snowman.
The Christmas miracle shines on
in the heart of the poorest child.
Away in the manger, Twelve Days of Christmas,
all the money we need . . .
Someone gives a gift, someone receive a gift,
brightly wrapped and be-ribboned,
passed out to the worthy and unworthy alike.
Still, some are passed over for reasons unknown.
Lack of money, lack of thought, of caring.
It only hurts for a moment before the numbness
sets in . . .
better to feel nothing than to feel unwanted.

ANOTHER YEAR

Another year has passed our tattered dreams
by the wayside.
Dreams, hopes, wishes,
all cast to the heavens
trickle down to earth, unrealized.
Aiming too high or too often, needs were not met.
Another year approaches another chance
to make things right, to make amends,
for slights real or imagined.

DAY PASS FROM THE ASYLUM

A taste of freedom, of a normal life,
a temporary respite from constraint.
Eight hours to breathe apart
from doctors, social workers.
Lunch, eaten out with family
who try to act as if everything is fine.
Conversations dance, lithe,
around uncomfortable topics,
never touching on the obvious.
Every comment soft, voices,
unfailingly cheery-having a false ring
to them.
You check the clock,
eager to return.

JANUARY COMMUTE

Frosty pillows around my car
sit at two feet high.
My booted feet plow through them
to leave a jagged scar.
There's a sheet of ice upon the windows
and the doors.
I scrape, I brush, I finally turn all defrosters on.
The car will warm up slowly now,
this frigid January.
Fleece and leather and down
will fend off the cold somehow.
The going's slow on icy roads
with high drifts on each side.
We pray for plows and salt trucks
delivering their loads.
Cars are in the median
who tried to move too fast
careened and swerved across the path
of those few driving free.
The troopers and the plow trucks
will have a busy day
to push, pull, tally up
those who've pressed their luck.

SHORT DAYS

Pristine tufts fall,
gathering on naked trees,
a flocking of white
against gray.
Skies, tarnished pewter,
collect as a backdrop
contrasting brilliant, sparkling patches
of irridescent cover.
Crystaline dunes ripple
amid frigid fields
spreading shimmer across bare acres
between snug houses, barns.
Flecks of intermittent blue
streak dour silver slabs
of cold sun and stack images
against a weakening day.

BUMP AND GRIND

Angry crags slash virgin drifts
with brown-gray decay,
ripped savagely by plows, cars.
Fragile fabric residue piles high,
obscuring the flow of life
on salt and cinder pitted avenues.
Clawing machines grab
burgeoning cliffs of snow,
slinging debris into gaping maws.
Tentative traffic travels at a respectable distance
within a seasonal bump and grind.

AS THE CROW FLIES

Starkest black
against curtains of silver.
Winter birds spread
sure wings against the day.
Endless spirals of feathed forms
travel well-rehearsed in the air.
Each flight
measured across the sky
to naked, waiting trees, taut wires.
Solitary aviators
find groups of kind
in welcoming clusters of fraternity.

OLD COUPLES

Sitting by the cozy fire,
bathed in soft light,
an old couple basks
in easy warmth.
Steady dog curled up
at their feet,
comfortable cat sleeping
on the grizzled mans lap.
A stack of well-read news papers
lean against his chair.
Gray hair piled on a nodding head,
the woman knits another scarf
for a familiar neck.
Night rolls peacefully for the pair,
near enough to be together
yet far enough to be alone.

THE JESUS IDEAL

Jesus is the ideal,
not the ideology;
not statuary in sweet rapose
or icon revered.
Even if the epitome of how
we should respond to one another . . .
Even if the belief is not in the man,
even if religion doesn't come into play,
adhering to a concept of kindness,
is the next best move.
A fellowship of understanding,
a kinship of love, a brotherhood of caring . . .
What it means to be a human being,
evolved from a central idea,
lessons sent across the ages
by good men, venerable women.
A wisdom rought in gentle purpose
dispersed to the masses-
not a belief but an action.

JANGLE BELLS

The phone rings.
A stabbing of the quiet night.
A piercing jangle of bells, of nerves
flaying the calm.
Who can it be?
You don't want to talk.
No matter who it is.
Wishing only eventual quiet,
you pick it up and wait for bad news.

SNOW DAYS

A scalding sun
this winter day
burns the bad moods right away.
Snowflakes glisten everywhere,
flashing light
in a seasons glow.
A sparkling down
hides any hint
of green grass
in iridescent glint.
Every task
we take in hand,
adorned by glitter
on the land.
The pristine shine
will melt away
in daylights effervescent rays.

DREAMS EMBRACE

When you visit in my dreams
I get to see your face.
I touch you with my soul
and time seems to erase.
I miss you so since you've been gone
these many aching years.
But, on occasion like this
I can wipe away my tears.
It's like you're really with me.
the images astound.
It seems to me you're really here,
that you're still around.
And, although I've known happy times
since you left this place,
I look forward to the moments
that I'm held in dreams embrace.

SEED COIN

Placed in your left pocket
to gather more in kind
a seed of gold is planted
with only good in mind.
Keep all ill away.
be positive and say
that you deserve the very best
that comes your way today.

LITTLE GIRL

Little girl
upon your grandpas knee,
he can see how beautiful
she will grow to be.
Little girl
gives the room a smile.
All attention turns her way
entrancing all the while.
Little girl
each day it seems you've grown.
Not quite the tiny baby
that we all have to known.
Little girl
your eyes are bright, your smile
lights up the room and gives
us sunshine for awhile.

THE GIFT

Son, you've given us a gift
a dollar cannot buy,
bundled in a blanket,
wrapped up in a sigh.
You gave us what we needed
as if you'd known all along,
echoed in a melody,
whispered in a song.
You've given us a treasure
to hold, to love, adore.
A gift from you, a gift from God.
We could not love them more.

A MOTHERS LOSS

To Bette S.

A heart, though empty, a room
filled with aching grief and gloom
with every sunrise brinks a doom-
it holds a mothers love.
Heart and soul a harbinger, a tomb,
empty as her ancient womb.
Weariness and sadness loom
above a Mothers loss.
The morning dove sings a forlorn tune,
resting in the trees at noon.
Waiting just one more full moon
to shine on a mothers loss.
With pain beyond all true belief
weighed down by a world of grief,
tears cried offer slight relief
flowing from a mothers loss.
No mere words can 'ere convey
the love of one who went away
The grief, the pain is there each day.
It is a mothers loss.
There is naught can hold a candle to
the loss of love that was so true.
there's nothing else that she can do
but accept a mothers loss.

SHE HAS NO REGRETS

From the moment she first held him in her arms
to the last time she saw him smile,
She has no regrets.
As she watched him grow
from baby to toddler to teen,
as she dreamed of the day he would marry,
bringing grandchildrento hold to her heart,
She has no regrets.
The love she gave to him
equaled the love he gave to her.
No day passed without a word of love
between them.
She has no regrets.
The day he left her embrace
suddenly, without fanfare or warning,
not by illness or war,
but anger, greed, evil . . .
for that she has regrets.
Another young man went to Hell,
to languish, safe from the woes of the world,
never see family again
as she will never see her son on this earth.
She has no regrets.

THE BIG STUFF

Every day life gets in the way of how we really feel.
From the kniggling of little peeves,
gnawing at us
to the slights setting us off balance.
We need to close our eyes,
go back to a time of calm,
a time of laughter, of joys.
We need to realize
that the small stuff need not erode
the love we have for the ones in our lives
who make up the big stuff.

APRILS SON

Aprils son
disolves in tears
that quell his incandescent fears
shining so as night time nears
and, he cannot sleep.
Somewhere, in a childs past,
damages were done
so no good thing seems to last
longer than a dream.
and so he eats, he sleeps his life away,
frustration always holding sway,
devouring the core of his day
as night goes on and on.
He cannot point to any blame
of any person he can name.
The pain is real, just the same.
He lives in the pain.

OH, SON OF MINE

Oh, son of mine,
you are a joy
even when things are bad,
when everything seems to be going wrong,
when it seems the world will end.
Even your mis-steps make me smile.
Mistakes make me grin
because I know how lucky I am
to have you for a son,
so glad to call you friend.
Eventhough your pockets are usually empty,
and you're looking for a loan,
or you need a hot shower,
there's a message that you send-
you need us
as much as we need you
to be there in a downturn,
in times of celebration-
all things family.

FORTUNES CHANGE

When life seems to ebb the lowest
and you round the curb of despair,
fortune, at last, smiles upon you
relinquishes your care.
When you're down to your last dollar.
When nothing makes much sense,
lady luck makes one mad dash
clearing every fence.
When your gas gauge reads passed empty
yet you still have miles to go,
you find a four-leaf clover
becoming luckier than you know.
When your dog barks and kid are crying,
when your spouse does naught but complain,
you get the break you have wished for
that keeps you from going insane.
When it seems that your fortunes are changing,
when you have better luck than you should,
tomorrow is another day
and not all luck is going to be good.
When all you touch turns to gold now
and you have that Midas touch,
you may garner the best and the brightest
of all that you've wanted so much.
So relish each turn of good fortune
when only pearls fall from your lips.
Hold tightly, enjoying the ride
that many more journey's eclipse.

OH, LITTLE ONES

Oh, little Ones
devouring life,
one gulp at a time.
Peels of laughter
ring the room
bouncing off the walls.
Smiles light up
even the gloomy places
hope shining through.
tiny arms wrap hugs
aroung weary shoulders
rejuvenating souls.

AM I BEAUTIFUL?

Am I beautiful?
asked by one so small
when beauty is the last thing
she should worry about.
Am I beautiful?
Can there be any doubt?
She is the truest beauty
both inside and out.
Am I beautiful?
The question should be moot.
When had insecurity
ever taken root?
Am I beautiful?
My, of course she is, by far.
She is my true beauty.
She is my shining star.
Am I beautiful?
She asks with quivering chin.
Tell her 'yes'
a hundred times.
I know she'll ask again.
Am I beautiful?
What more can I say?
She's as beautiful as the sun.
She brightens up my day.
Am I beautiful?
Dear, where can I start?
She is the most beautiful because
of the beauty in her heart.

FATHERS ARE

Fathers are the root of the family tree,
they are the anchor to the earth.
Father joins mother in support,
a bridge between the world and home.
Fathers undestand how hard to throw a ball,
how to dunk, how to kick, how to punt.
Fathers know accidents happen
and are there to help out.
Fathers are the life blood,
filling the veins of his children.
In adulthood, he is thier heart.
Fathers carry the gaunlet
where mothers cannot-
in the rough and tumble world.
Ask who's important-
fathers are.

MOTHERS ARE

Mothers are the heartbeat
of the family, the rythm.
Mothers are the balm of wounds
making all things better.
Mothers nurture, cuddle, cook;
stand firm, negotiate, give in.
Mothers know what's best,
give their all, accept and give in love.
Mothers know sometimes
a cookie cures all.
Mothers are the soul that makes
a house a home.
When asked who's important-
mothers are.

CHILDREN

The joy of small things
light a childs eyes.
Smiles warm even cold hearts with wonder.
A firefly in the dusky sky,
a bumble bee buzzing near
a flower,
a bird building a nest, a puppys cold nose,
a contented kittens purr . . .
all catch the attention of a child.
Their laughter, so infectious,
brings the maudlin back to joy
in one quick burst.
The hope of our tomorrows-children-
they are what they learn of us, Use care.

I WAS SICK

See, I told you I was sick!
She speaks as she is dying.
The other doctors were too quick.
They thought that she was lying.
She took every known elixor,
swallowed each and every pill.
Who would have guessed indifference
would break her iron will?
She went to the doctors office
to get a quick exam.
the doctor asked her "Are you sick?"
She answered :"Yes, I am."
She sat down on the table.
The doctor said "Don't Cry."
"I don't know how to say this,
but, I believe you're going to die."
She looked him in the eye.
She answered. She was quick.
"Could I have that in writing?
See I told you I was sick!"

SUMMER BURST

Rain pelts the sweating pavement.
Steam rises, a heady vapor,
cloying yet refreshing.
Blades bend as drops drum the ground.
Music pounds the concrete.
Rythm breaks in time to the beat
of precipitation.
Steady rudiments of a summer song
punctuated by thunder, lightening.
Clouds separate dark from light,
allowing sky to peak through.

TIME FLIES

The strangest thing occured to me
just the other day-
when I look into the mirror,
should I be seeing gray?
Birthdays seem to fly these days.
It seems like such a bother.
Just when you're set to celebrate,
it's time to have another.
I went to bed at twenty-one,
when I woke up, I was thirty.
Age is playing tricks on me
and every one is dirty!
Just as I was used to forty,
that era ceased to be.
I woke up past fifty,
eligible for A.A. R.P.
Now I sit, past fifty-five,
wondering how I dare.
Just sit back, relax
and wait for Medicare.

MY BABY

My baby's grown now, he's a man
with a family of his own.
He does all that is expected of him
plus a little extra.
Up before the sun to work
he spends his day with those of his ilk.
When he walks home,
his wife is there to regale him with
the days events,
Children wake from napping
to come to his open arms.
After dinner, dishes, he has reflective time-
a walk, stroller in front with one of the tykes.
he walks down to see his dad and I,
share smoke and a soda.
He'll outline happenings,
ponder the meaning of all things
before he heads home.
He's grown up.
We couldn't be more proud.
But . . . he's still my baby.

TO LEE, ON HIS WAY

Where has the time flown?
You're grown!
The day we all found out you were on your way,
your mom and sisters had pie to celebrate.
Everyone was ready, you were anticipated.
A child on the horizons whose gifts
would fill thw world with good.
You've spent the years growing
into the man we knew you would be.
Now, we gather together to say good-bye,
to share you with humanity, to know
your wonderful epiphany.
You will spread your warmth to a distant
land, urging new growth among the young.
A tableau is set before you with vibrant mornings
to greet you, sweet winds to whisper
around you, enchanting sunsets to keep you safe.
New friends will enrich you while absence
will intensify our appreciation of you at home.
You will do good things, nephew.
You are a good man.
We're all so proud of you.
You stand at the apex of your future
through a welcoming portal to vistas
unimagined.
What happens tomorrow and after,
will mold your destiny.
We love you, Lee.

RIVER OF TIME

The river wears us smooth . . .
we are just so many bits of glass,
pebbles picked up and carried through time.
From top to bottom,
we struggle against currents,
trying in vain to hold our place,
to keep forward progress in check.
The river is too strong.
For all our best efforts, we tumble along
with debris, eddying to the side of
the water.
Rivlets trickle shamelessly, combining
torrents, roaring.
Rivers of life flow until we meet
in the vastness of oceans.

LIFE GOES ON

We are flotsom, debris,
wave-tossed on lifes open seas.
Water is as endless as life.
It is ongoing,
self-perpetuating.
Water begets water, begets life.
Life may end, but in that end,
is a new beginning, another kind of life.

WE NEVER SAY GOOD-BYE

When we say "good-bye",
part of our heart holds on.
We never truly let go.
Some small part of our soul stays in contact,
through the distance.
We never lose touch, not really.
Time, space may rift chasms
but are never beyond encroachment.
In thoughts, in dreams,
the missing visit, revisiting old feelings.
Love dies a slow death . . . not days, weeks;
not months years, decades . . . maybe never.
Moving on doesn't mean moving away.
We stay close, physicall, spiritually.
The distance is moot.
We are as close as a heartbeat
from a breath.
As visible as a blink to a glance.
Weary composite memories . . .
Our mind full of re-touched images
of old loves, old homes . . . anything
we have loved and lost.
To encounter these essences,
we would find them changed but our
hearts would enjoy reunions.
We never really say 'good-bye'.

GRAY FRIDAY

Gray day
the world rouses slowly,
The sun, eyes half-open,
rest far from bedroom windows.
Sleepers wake late.
Folks ready for their day,
promises bleak.
Fine mist drifts across
windshields as workers make
their way.

PROMISE

Skies promise rains eventually
Storms rush over lakes,
churning with fullness.
Only man goes forth.
Animals stay close until
weather passes.

SLEEPY DAY

Sleepy summer day . . .
gray, misty, cool . . .
the world seems adaze,
suspended in slow motion,
abbreviated, hesitating, a bit behind.
Stray cats meader, house dogs loll about,
pausing but not stopping.

OCTOBER MORNING

Deep into morning that brinks dark, wet,
I dodge raindrops, kick through golden
leaves to my car.
Windshield wipers clap in time to the
drops splattering the glass.
Streets are patent-leather dark,
glassy with a dangerous sheen to
the pavement.
Darkness so deep it engulfs my field
of vision-road, horizon indistinguishable.
As the sky takes light, the road becomes
distinct,
the way less treacherous.

MORNING RITUAL

I tumble out of bed each day
performing my routine.
Looking in my bathroom mirror
is the biggest mess I've seen.
My hair sticks up, my face is creased;
I'm pale, I'm gaunt, I'm wan.
I wash my face, I brush my teeth
and someone I go on.
I trundle to the kitchen where
my coffee pot sits still
knowing my redemtion waits
for the pot to fill.
The full aroma fills the air
as steam rises up
summoning a steady hand
to fill my coffee cup.
I lift the cup in both my hands
hold it to my lips.
The rest is but a ritual
I have learned by rote.
I swirl the nectar ore my tongue
and down my eager throat.
I get a smooth, warm feeling
and I know no other way
to warm my soul and wake me so
I can begin my day.

PASSPORT

A book opens to more than a brief, printed page.
It is a portal to another time, another place.
Between maleable covers
harkening mystery, adventure.
We burrow into characters,
living through their experiences,
caught up in the mixture of images
conjured by words.
Old or young, rich or poor,
all are transported to the realm of imagination
where beggers become kings and love endures
all.
We may travel at our leisure merely closing the book
to delay our journey;
only needing to begin again to continue the trip.

UNTOUCHABLES

Gathering in clusters at the perimeter
of buildings,
the new perreha smokes the time away,
butts gripped between finger and thumb,
sucking every molecule through stained fingers.
Plumes of vapor escape nostrils as smokers converse
between drags.
As traits garnered to belong now excludes,
suffering sin tax, price embargos,
reminiscent of the cool kids at the edges
of the yard just beyond school property,
enduring the vagaries of weather to enjoy their habits.

SUMMERS LAST HURRAH

Spun sugar skies, mauve, rose
stretch across horizons.
Naked limbs clutch an ethereal presence
as summer grapples for one last hurrah
passed autumn.
Balmy breezes haunt heady days
of temperance.
It cannot last.
We wish it would not escort snows,
stage left.
Changing seasons rock the night
of frost and fog.
(just enough to coax sleeping lovers
close beneath blankets.)
Evergreens applaud their sole position
of green in a brown gold world.
Skeletal trees wave mute salutations
to the world, whispering hushed, rustling tones;
lamenting changes to come.

BROTHERHOOD

It's been so long
since you've been near.
We've seen changes in our lives.
We've grown apart, I fear.
Your hair is gray,
a framed face aged.
Your spirit soars free,
your soul uncaged.
You search for answers
to fill your book of dreams
but memories and family
both pull at the seams
of this frayed and fragile vessel
where we find ourselves ensnared
by actions, by the motives
of those who said they cared.
Bound by blood and sorrow,
our journies mark the places
etched in lines and shadows
on our familiar faces.

WRECKAGE

Once there was a little boy,
blue eyes, rosey cheeks.
Now, he is a man, he's grown.
It is the answers that he seeks.
His tossled head was torn away
from his mothers breast,
left in th care of grandma
with his sister and the rest.
Three little boys who needed care,
a gentle place to land
were scolded and were frightened
by their grandmas hand.
She scrubbed them down with Oxydol
until their skin was raw-
just dirty little Tisdales-
that is all she saw.
They were quiet, they were hungry;
they were patient and so sad.
She gave the older brothers
over to their dad.
The little one, she kept awhile
until one day by phone
she found a 'real nice couple'
to give the boy a home.
As quickly as a puppy
adopted from the pound,
they took him to their busom.
He never made a sound.
He stayed with them awhile until
on a sparkling summer day,
his mother raced down that country road
and snatched the boy away.
It broke a loving family
who took him as their own

but a mother can be righteous
in pursuit of flesh and bone.
She didn't take the girl.
She didn't take the older boys.
The little men had many trials,
The girl just had her toys.
Every child she touched has suffered
from that very day,
flung from pillar to any post
because she could not stay.

THANKSGIVING WISH

A family gathers to remember
good times throughout the year,
to be with loved ones once again
who come from far and near.
HAnds clasped around the table,
we count our blessings then.
Giving thanks for bounty,
we can count them all again.
Passing food from left to right
to fill our waiting plate
in turn to fill each belly,
our appetites to sate.
As each one of us gives thanks
on this thursday in November,
think of those who do without
then try to remember
there but for the grace of God
you could have an empty dish,
recalling those less fortunate
with your thanksgiving wish.

REMEMBER THE 'GIVE' IN THANKSGIVING

Before each slice of pumpkin pie,
each piece of roasted meat,
let thoughts go to those with less
before you take your seat.
As you look from face-to-face
with love, your family
will fill the void left all year round
when time is not so free;
when jobs and cares fill everyday,
when troubles seem the worst;
We realize on holidays
that family should come first.
It is not your mom, your dad,
your sister of your wife-
it's all your friends and neighbors
who give meaning to your life.
So share your joy with others
as you go to take your seat
Put the 'give' in your Thanksgiving
with the circle now complete.

NONE THE WORSE FOR THE GIVING

The greater the gift is the giving,
the greater the giving the act,
an integral part of the living,
the gift is a matter of fact.
The greater the life is the purpose,
the greater the purpose to live;
the blessing or the curse is
your willingness to give.
The greater the gifts, the receiving
to receive is an equal command
of the Lord when he was conceiving
give to receive the demand.
For every one thing given out,
two things to be is its place,
will make more room for the grace.
If your coffers seem too empty to
give freely, as you care,
just reach a little deeper you
will find a bounty there.
Give one coin, get three back,
multiples return
following every generous act
with interest that you earn.
Embrace the charitable, indulge
empty pockets, purse.
They will fill until they bulge
and you'll feel none the worse.

ANOTHER YEAR

Another year,
I have survived
this farce called life
somewhat contrived.
Anothr year
and I still breathe;
I walk, I smile, I love
and so bequeathe
Another year,
to share with those
I know, I love, I met on paths
no other chose.
Another year,
I am still here
My life, my being shared
with all that I hold dear.
Another year,
let me exhale
each happy thing to those
I've met
so they may hear my tale.
Another year,
as more will see
waiting for all to live
for eager eyes to see
Another year
I'm here I last
I have endured my fall from grace
(it happened very fast)
Another yer
to know another sun
to live each day asif
it were my last one.

JUST ANOTHER DAY

On my birthday there
will be no cake
just wrinkled skin
and bones that ache.
There'll be no silly games to play.
You see, November 28th
is just another day.

FAITH

To have faith unshakeable
To believe that wrongs will be set right
by virtue of a few select words intoned
by someone or something
larger than life.
It would be easier in life
to have that thought process,
that God's will pre-ordained, the outcome,
negating our responsibility in the mess called life,
this immutable faith not my own.
I have my doubts a good and caring God
would be so impetuous.
but, what do I know?

PRAYER

A prayer
an incantation
carefully chosen syllables offered up
in hope of bringing change
A chant
a hymn
a war dance
stirring up the ether waves.
Positive affirmations . . .
It shouldn't make a difference
these conversations with ourselves
Common sense dictates
that it shouldn't work!
Mere protestations of 'OH God'
as we enjoin to be delivered
from our problems,
recitation
eventually, something changes
it shouldn't work
but it does.

CALL IT WHAT YOU WILL

We murmur
to pull ourselves from thoughts
of dipair.
We think positive thoughts,
a little cheerleading exercise
will lift us.
We pray
pulling at celestial straws
for a better outcome.
The universe is listening-
call it what you will-
a wish, unspoken, will never come true.
Our utterances draw on eternity,
waves of energy from beyond the beyond,
waiitng to hear from us
to set the cogs for change.

WHAT CAME FIRST

That spark of life
a kernal of being,
set on a path of generation.
What came first?
Does it matter?
Molecules unite, divide forming mass.
Mass develops according to its
genetic blue print,
cats become cats,
people, people
or so we are led to believe.
What happens when there is a glitch
in the universe?
A mistake takes shape
a mental, a physical monstrosity,
a form hard to gaze upon,
a thought process foriegn
to the norm . . .
how does it happen?
What came first?

BABY'S FIRST CHRISTMAS

Children wonder always about Christmas day,
tearing through the packages,
they sit in disarray.
But, on that one first Christmas
it's everything it seems for the parent, for the child
a culminating dream.
In awe of all the beauty,
the color and glitter.
they sit stunned and silent
amid the Christmas litter.
They open up the boxes
that hold the shiny toys;
bright and bold and gaudy,
making lots of noise.
Their eyes are wide, their little mouths
are drawn up in a bow.
Slowly their first Christmas is
the best they'll ever know.
When all the paper's picked up
and the babe is fast asleep
Hold that image in your memory
where it is yours to keep.

CHRISTMAS DAY

A fresh snow fell last evening.
The world's wash with white.
Colored lights of the season glisten
sparkling in the night.
The childen build their snowmen,
bundled up so warm,
they move like little robots
with fleece and down the norm.
Moms are baking cookies now.
The dads are wrapping gifts.
(It's the giving not receiving
that makes the spirits lift.)
The Christmas cards are in the mail,
the kids have made their lists.
Sister's under the mistle toe
waiting to be kissed.
Colored papers, shiny bows
a-tumble by the tree
twinkling lights and ornaments
for everyone to see.
Smells of cooking fill the air,
the turkey and the stuffing
reward us for the shovling,
the huffing and the puffing.
The wassail bowl, the smooth egg nog
really hit the spot.
There are many signs of Christmas
yet many things it's not.
It isn't greed or avarice;
keep selfish thoughts away.
Give until it just feels right
every Christmas day.

FROM METRO I

A plume of vapors undulates from the ground,
vented to the world.
Spreading, it envelopes the air itself.
Clinging to bodies, buildings.
It hangs from denuded trees,
a ghostly mass for the ages.
Breathe deep, my fellow travelers.
tkae in the chemicals that make
the modern man.

FROM METRO II

Sunshine, cataclysmic, bursts from the clouds,
exploding through the grimy windows,
atomic aftermath.
Shreds of cotton filter the light,
traveling increments across the sky.
A patch of pure blue swathed in white
beckons to workers, welcoming them on their journey home.
Gray shuffles through
addressing the brief change.
The sun is at a place of brilliant possibilities,
a momentary flash of warmth
on a winter afternoon.
Too soon it will drift behind the darker clouds
to shine on the night and its luminaries.

ODE TO THE GOOD PEOPLE

The skyline brinks hazy, grim.
Stark trees, grasping, naked limbs
reach heavenward.
The good people of the world
park their cars in concrte behemouths.
Walking to their jobs, they are thinking of other things
to spend their time on-
things that pay just as well
only not in coin, but in laughter, joy, fellowship . . .
Perhaps the payoff is long in coming
but they toil on.
Each smile is chattle that fills their pocket,
jangling laughter.
The parking lots are full, cars waiting, forelorn.
When the work day ends,
the horizons alight with people
going where they'd rather be.

ONE LONE MAN

One lone man
walks the walk,
head down, hands in his pockets.
A terrible weight bears down on him.
There is plenty of room
in his empty pockets for his hands.
There is plenty of room in his hungry belly.
Times are not good for him.
He wants.
He needs.
He languishes apart from the world.

FROM METRO III

Today, the sunshine.
Blue skies trimmed by tufts of white . . .
cars stream steadily down the highway.
People on their way to their lives . . .
Bare trees stand stark against a
back drop of concrete.
A solitary bird takes wing against the day.

OH, CAPTAIN

I am the captain of my ship.
My course, charted by my own hand.
I watch for storms, for warnings;
for waters too shallow or deep.
breaking shoals may lie ahead.
My true north rests within.
Rough currents to whirling eddies
wait for me.
Bouys mark a sure path if I am watchful.

I WISH

I wish I could afford to buy a gift
for the world.
To wrap them all up gaily,
with bright ribbons,
tying them by the heartstrings
to bind us, one and all,
as a family for one season, to lift us, to elate us,
for just one night-a union of joy, of hope, of love . . .

THE GIFT

You have given me so much,
a box could never hold.
No paper could wrap, no ribbon bind.
I filled a void so long ago,
so vast, in a world co cold
because you were so kind.

JUNE DUSK

Verigated veils drop deflty,
amethyst, blush, blue
falling, now, a curtain
before the slipping day.
Dusty ribbons swathe horizons
bidding day to rest.
Soft hues swaddle clouds
binding deepening skies.
Hushed lullabys breathe into the night
embracing weary twilight,
rocking us in cooling arms-
one world asleep, another awakening.

LONG RIDE HOME

headlights rim the distant curves ahead.
Amish buggies flash and jag,
interspersed with cars, trucks.
It's a long, quiet ride home.
Careful not to speed,
a song plays in my head.
Orange signs punctuate
the untrimmed shoulder of the route,
promising delay.
Late sun shoots through
the corner of the window.
I keep a steady rythm at ten and two.
Passing hand painted advertisements
extolling goatmilk fudge, farm fresh eggs.
It is a quiet ride,
chewing up tires, inhaling gasoline.
Home soon.

TAPESTRY

A tapestry of life,
our countenance bears testimony
of our journies.
A deliberately stitched cloth
worked over time.
Each smile, every sadness
chronicled on the fragile sampler
of our days.

GOOD MORNING

Broaching light ushers morning song,
filling tree tops.
Pulling curtains reveal the veil of night,
lifting trepidaciously.
Colors ebb the sky, pushing
at darker edges of horizons,
letting in light.
Slight sun catches glints of dew
on clipped grass.
Birds hop, breakfasting on succulent worms,
industrious early on.
Slowly, doors open.
Hands grope in half-light
for morning papers while coffee brews inside.
House dogs strut on taut leashes
as cars flow into traffic.
Slowly, the world stretches, humanity yawns, wakes.

BEFORE WE REST

Heaven lifts its veil to let us in,
joined in ecstasy of spirit.
Deep embracing shadows
shroud the room.
Prayerfully, we rest,
with utterances to God.
Lifting exhaltations
to heights new to rapture.
Slowly,
the world encroaches bliss.
We rest.

THE QUEST

Electric earth fire touches
some secret places
known only in dreams;
lifting levels unobtainable alone.
Solemn chasms fill to glowing, ecstatic
illumination.
Rising, souls reach deep into psyches,
seeking self-knowledge-
a query unabated by thought.
In second sight,
memory eclipses recollection of the blind eye.

EARLY JUNE DAYS

June eases into summer days,
blues slipping subtly from grays.
Temporate skies absorb the rays
of warmer moments in the sun.
Flowers burst into full bloom,
chasing out pre-summer gloom.
Petals spread, leaves make room
with gardeners efforts glad.
Day birds trill a garden refrain,
delighting after days of rain
to pull worms from ground again
for their joyous feast.
Little girls with basketballs,
boys in tattered overalls
listen as their mother calls
as days draw to a close.
Dinner and the dishes done,
bathroom battles fought and won
with the setting of the sun
now time is at its rest.

FATHERS DAY

from the moment he first held you
he knew what you were worth-
value given by his heart
the moment of your birth.

NICK'S DAD

A small bundled miracle, he held you,
fresh from heaven, from the doctors hands.
He knew his days would be fulfilled
as you grew to be a man.
He watched you grow,
he held you close,
yet, he let you follow free,
learning all you could from life
how each day should be.
There were ball games,
there were hospital stays,
times when you both were sick . . .
of all the good, the bad of them,
there's one that he would pick . . .
the day you held within your arms
your own treasured, tiny son.
Your dad knew that the torch had passed.
Now, his job was done.

MISSING DAD

Dad's gone awhile, now, since 1999.
There's not a moment past when I regret
he was my dad.
I wish I could go back to his house,
sit down, have a beer.
I envy all the folks my age
who have their fathers still.
No more wise, no more caring words
will drift passed my ear.
All I have are memories
of my dad that I hold dear.
His blood shot eyes, the morning stubble
spread across his face . . .
I sure do miss my dear dad
since he has left this place.
There aren't many pictures left.
No albums set apart.
All my memories collect
here, within my daughters heart.

GRAY HAIR THERE

"Age is mind over matter. If you don't mind, it don't matter."
Somewhere in my dyed red hair
there lurks a hair so gray
when I finally find it,
it will ruin my whole day.
I've come to terms
with granny flaps,
with wrinkles, cellulite . . .
when I saw that gray hair there
I nearly died of fright!
I'd read once in Playboy
a lass must match collar/cuff.
I saw no gray hairs on my head,
only in my muff!
The puffy bags beneath my eyes-
character, etched so fine,
my forehead, eyes, my mouth
are, by rights, all mine.
I never did have freckles
now, I have liver spots.
Sometimes I play a mental game
and just connect the dots.
I've given up all thoughts of tan.

I'm alabaster white.
I was under black light yesterday
and I was quite a sight.
But what really makes my age creep up
into my constant view-
my oldest daughter showed me
that she has gray hair, too.
But as I truly see it,
all thingd being sound,
I'd happily live forever
as long as I can move around.
With walker, cane or wheelchair
adorned by my gray hair
Don't pull the plug if everything
is working under there.

OPEN DOOR

Do you have a secret
I should know about.
You wonder if I truly care
when there should be no doubt.
Chunks of time doled out to us,
stolen from the masses,
enjoyed to the very fullest
before the hour passes.
A slice of day, a bit of night,
we garner what we can,
securing what we might.
The music plays,
the song endures.
When I ache for company
I'm hoping that it's yours.
Our minutes are so precious.
We must try to glean
every fleeting nuance
that we catch in between.
Time flys so swiftly
the days pile up before
it's time to spend the afternoon
inside your open door.

A GAP IN DESTINY

Words in the body of a song
drift into reality.
Each verse tells a tale of longing, need, woe.
A story concealed within the notes.
Yet, known to any who care to listen.
Unlikely friends that make sense together,
telling the world, telling themselves.
Music plays across miles
filling hours, days
bridging a gap in destiny.

UNCLE BILL NEVER LAUGHED ENOUGH

Uncle Bill
never laughed enough
but, when he did,
the joy burst from his soul, unencumbered.
A raucous, voluptuous huge gaffaw-
all rapture and music.
His mirth would trill,
an exotic jungle bird,
full of life, color, rich . . .
To hear him so
would illuminate the room, the house, the world.
What clever turn caused the explosion, emotion
to eclipse sullen, serious sides?
Generous, true, jewel-like
from his lips, his lungs, his laugh . . .
Uncle Bill never laughed enough.

DAD TILLED THE EARTH

Dad tilled the earth until
a deep, soft, rich loam
spread perfume, wafting throughout.
Dad tilled the earth
mixed dirt and manure
to a dark combo
for fine planting.
Dad tilled the earth,
each seed dropped easily
from weathered grip,
never carelessly scattered
One after another,
straight, elegant in its simplicity,
it regularity.
Dad tilled the earth,
yielding all he planted, cared for
everyday with tiller. with water, sweat.
Dad tilled the earth,
urged it, producing
with the aid of the sun, rain,
perseverance.
Dad tilled the earth;
finishing, he rested
on the empty wagon of his tiller,
wiping his brow with a blue kerchief.
Dad tilled the earth;
I learned from him
to give the earth
love, caring understanding;
a respect, knowing
that the earth cannot give alone
Dad tilled the earth . . .

THIS IS THE WAY

This is the way she did her wash
every monday
into two metal tubs
stirring boiling water
with big sticks.
Scrubbing, cracked fingers on a board
One piece after another through the wringer,
water squeezing into a another galvanized basin.
All year long, bleeding knuckles
bending with wooden pins attaching
cloths, sheets to a rope line
inside out.
Off the line, ready for ironing.
No bleach, no softener, no static cling;
just fresh, clean smelling laundry
smelling of sun and fresh air.
This is the way she does her wash

WHAT FUN WE HAD

What fun we had
in our 1959 gray Ford wagon

All kids piled in the back,
sitting on the lowered tail gate,
eating BIG banana popcicles.

What fun we had

Before seat belts and child restraints-
dirt and rocks dancing at our summer feet
as we cruised back roads.

What fun we had

Leaning out from open crank-down windows,
reaching for passing tree branches
whipping at our open, laughing faces.

What fun we had

Riding up an d down hills so fast
our bellies would jump, lifting as we screamed
"wheeeeee!"

What fun we had.

MEMORIES LIKE THESE

When raspberries are ready, ripe,
sometime in July,
Corn so green, stalks so supple,
'so high by the fourth of July' . . .
Memories fill my summer days
Memories like these.
We'd trek with our wooden baskets
up and down each row,
loading bumpy succulents,
eating more than we'd show.
Memories fill my summer days,
Memories like these.
We would earn a big 10 cents
for every quart we'd pick.
Sun and sand and berrie bushes
that would whip and prick.
Memories fill my summer days,
Memories like these.
Every day we'd tally
what our efforts earned,
take off our shoes, turn our heads
to see if we'd been burned.
Memories fill our summer days,
Memories like these.
That was a Welton summer
when I was very young.

The land whispered melodies
that are no longer sung.
We are not the family
who labored side-by-side
or clammored at our uncle Bill
begging for a ride;
who sat around the table
beneath the sumac trees.
I treasure what they left to me,
great memories like these.
Memories fill my summer days,
memories like these.

TINY, SHINY SHARDS

Every weekend, we'd gather
for dinner, picnics, cards.
Those are fragile memories, like glass,
in tiny, shiny shards.
The kids would all play chidish games.
Uncle Bill might play along.
Ma would sit out on the porch
regaling us with song.
Pa, in gray, would sit and spit;
placid, he'd look on.
I don't know these people, now.
I wonder where they've gone?
Nancy, Linda, Uncle Bill;Aunt Babe
and Uncle Paul; Aunt Leta, Ma and of course, Pa-
I miss them one and all.
Some are gone forever.
Some, are just plain gone.
Though they will not be recognized,
these memories live on.
We are still a family
and if push came to shove,
I think they'd all have to admit
there was a lot of love.
each of these missing pieces
has a special place
that the friends and family
of today cannot replace.
There is a section of my heart
where my memories reside
of a life when full,
when family had a softer side.
But they've shattered like so much broken glass
in many a tiny, shiny shard.
I won't give up my memories,
the grief would hit too hard.

FAT AND SKINNY HAD A RACE

I was the fat/skinny kid,
when younger then when older.
The anger and the hurt swell up.
My feelings burn and smolder.
I was the butt of many jokes,
I'd cry.
No slight, no indignation
would easily slip by.
I just could never get it right,
even going fat to thin.
My family had its own small grooves.
I never did fit in.
I'd never stare into a mirror.
I'd never take a look.
It was just much easier to be buried in a book.
My imaginationsaved me;
my music, boooks, my horse.
Everything I learned to do,
was ignored, of course.
I bring home a big, blue ribbon,
get the lead part in the play.
"Well" they say "Meryl, did you cheat to get your way?"
I never heard a word from them-
no compliments, no praise-
only laughing insults
filled my younger days.
I miss uncle Bills hearty laugh.
I miss dads churly cough.
I miss them all but now I know
I'm really better off.
I can do without the digs.
I don't need their decree.
I don't need their acceptance
of who I've grown to be.

OH, DAUGHTER

Oh, daughter, how we do talk now.
We share our lives, our story
Never wasting precious time
saying that we're sorry.
Oh, daughter, how we do talk now.
With many things to share.
We let the past just slip on by.
Hardly worth our care.
Oh, daughter, how we do talk now.
Our lives run parallel.
We've traveled on our journey,
each through a separate Hell.
Oh, daughter, how we do talk now.
We have healed the rift.
We've mended all our fences
and it's been a real gift.
Oh, daughter, how we do talk now.
We march to the same song.
We learn of love, of family
as we go along.
Oh, daughter, how we do talk now.
Age garners recompense,
As mothers, what we say and do
finally makes sense.
Oh, daughter, how we do talk now.
Our children are above
through any aspect of their lives,
they will always have our love.
Oh, daughter, how we do talk now.
I share, you share what's in you.
Throughout our time on earth I hope
our talks will long continue.

BIG IS BEAUTIFUL

Elandra, as your grandmother,
I must do my duty
to assure you that you truly are
a genuine young beauty.
Tall, so statuesque, you stand.
You always are a joy.
Before too long you will adorn
the arm of some lucky boy.
You're smart, your talent is so great
that many recommend
we share you with the masses
and the message that they send
should tell you how you rise above,
that you are a sage
eclipsing any other girl
or boy that is your age.
Let Pride be in your bearing.
It's not concrete at all.
Head held high, how you're treated,
will likely be your call.
Keep your shoulders back, stand tall.
Keep both eyes straight ahead.
Over shadow tiny and petite.
Be big and beautiful instead!

CURTS LOVING ARMS

It was a blessing to our family
when he came into her life
again after so many years
and made our girl his wife.
The godess graced her with a love
that would pass the test,
that lifts her to the pinnacle
so far above the rest.
Some before had held her down
to keep her in her place.
It grieved us all to see the tears
stream down her pretty face.
She has found happipness, at last,
and life, now, has its charms.
She's safe, now, she can finally rest
within Curts loving arms.

MUSIC IN THE RAIN

Syncopated
wipers thrum across glass,
slashing side-to-side.
Roads and sky
match grays
slick as glass
with smokey edges.
Grass bends on the roadside,
weighed down
by heaving drops.
Incessant rythms strike
a melody on the car top
as I drive.
The radio is on
but the real music
is in the rain.

A CREATURE OF GODS HAND

A horse, magical, a creature struck in beauty by God,
unpredictably trustworthy as a friend.
Bearing riders with pride
as if all men were kings,
traveling on.
Sacrificing comfort to give pleasure,
transporting physically, spiritually,
calmimg, amusing, endearing.
No greater love by any beast for a master,
giving when seemingly nothing left.
A spirit unending, enduring,
the essence of nobility.

A WOMAN CALLED VALOR

Tree dancer, horse lover, cat fancier . . .
my friend,
genuine, quietly caring,
woman born of pain.
Giving, sacrificing, real.
Never pretending what she could never be.
Dancing a joyous dervish in the forest,
having the bearing of a queen on horseback.
Always tender to all creatures.
I am proud to call her friend.

THEY SAY THEY DON'T LIKE CATS

Whoever says they don't like cats
never saw two kittens play
or knew a cat who could stretch out
on a window ledge all day.
They can have never noticed
a mother with her young
so nurturing, so caring, teaching
just as life's begun.
They never witnessed community
of cats numbering more than two
or how they pay attention to everything you do.
Cats can teach mere humans
about true family.
The man who doesn't like a cat
hasn't seen the cats I've seen.

COTTON CANDY SKIES

Spun sugar sunsets
smooth the horizon.
gracefully, day ends.

Verigated skies embrace
late climbing clouds
setting the stage for night.

Sun slowly eases past our sight
night birds in the shadows
echo lullabyes to the world.

SPENDTHRIFT

June pulls her purse strigs,
closing summer slowly
as the day begins a shorter span
easing into inevitable fall.
Just begun,
yet nearly gone . . .
Plants grow, rains fall, lawns need mowing.
two more months of summer
before autumn.
Yet, we spend our days
long before we have lived them.

AFTERGLOW

Stars fall to earth,
down from indigo heights,
shining brightly for a time.
The most brilliant
will shine, flare, then die away
somewhere in the heavens.

PRAGMATIC SON

He holds his faith tightly, in a clenched fist.
Always needing to see, feel, to know for a fact.
If he can see it, taste it, feel it,
it must be real.
What of love? What of trust?
What of things known to the heart?the soul?
Pragmatism is a double-edged sword . . .
everything proven, concrete, definitive.
But, there must be room for the fantastic,
the magical . . .
What of dreams?
Hold faith in an open hand.
Feel the truth of the soul, of love, of dreams.
Believe in the love of one another.
Trust tomorrow will follow today.
Breathe magic into the world.

PARENT TRAP

Each babe that softly sleeps today
will one day come of age,
facing us with torments of adolescent rage.
Our motives will be misconstrued.
They will never understand
our reasons for restrictions
or all that we demand.
Their comments, accusations
will cut us to the bone.
Rest assured. they'll understand
when they've children of their own.
All parents are quite unprepared
as time drops in their lap
recriminations and regrets . . .
the real parent trap.

WHAT WE REAP

Somedays it seems we wait for God
to drop the other shoe.
We know that we're accountable
for what we say and do.
Whatever sound escapes our lips
we must be ready to defend;
actions, words, emotions
that carelessness may rend.

ESTEEMED RESPECT

Children are all-knowing
when it comes to our mistakes.
Any inconsistency
will be all that it takes
to take the glow off their respect
and make us seem quite less
than we once were in their esteem
encouraging redress.
Our children, then, will understand
with our cards laid on the table.
They'll sense the right, the truth, what's real
every nuance every variable.
To hold acclaim within their eyes
we must face as fact
our truthfulness, our honesty,
our veracity, our tact.

*___

LAMENTATIONS OF A PATIENT

What will I do when you have gone?
Where am I to go
to shed my soul of sorrow
when no one else can know
the heartaches and the nightmares
and the weaknesses that show?
What will I do when you have gone?
Where am I to go
to share my many troubles
with, whom will I share
all my hopes, my dreams, my fears?
Who else is there to care
if I have troubling visions
that haunt me from out there
with ghosts, with sprites, with demons
to vex and plague me so?
What will I do when you have gone?
Where am I to go
to receive salvations balm
to get absolution from
when the fires of Hell rage on,
when all the devils come,
I must admit it bothers me,
that I worry some
about who extends a hand to me . . .
what will I become?
What will I do when you have gone?
Where am I to go?
If I hold back,
if I shut down,
I guess I'll never know
where to get the help I need
that's where I'll have to go.

WE'LL TAKE YOU BACK

If your ambitious plans collapse
and your dreams fall of track,
turn around and head our way.
We'll gladly take you back.
If your highest hopes are dashed
and your illusions lack
the sustainance to see you through,
we'll gladly take you back.
If your life becomes too boring
or you're under times attack,
turn around, come our way,
We'll gladly take you back.
If your goals are far from being met
and your soul's stretched on the rack,
rest assured, we are still there.
We'll always take you back.

OHIO'S HEAT

Drawn into the vortex
of Ohio's heat,
humidity envelopes us
from pate down to our feet.
The air is close, so cloying;
labored breaths repeat.
Winds are non-existent
as we're sticking to our seat.
Mid-day sun burns from above,
scorching asphalt and concrete;
shining like Gods ego
in celestial conceit.
We wait for late afternoon
with temperatures replete
of damp and stinging mugginess,
where time and comfort meet.

OHIO IN JULY

A noon day sky of fairest blue,
mottled by tufts of drifting white,
embrace a torrid firmament,
sun ablaze upon the suffering.
Necks damp, clothes clinging;
sour smells of old activity
linger rancid, as people pass by,
glistening with sweat.
Gardens, lawns beg respite.
Flowers dip and curl in supplication
to a rain slow to arrive,
barely quenching parched masses.
Shaded eyes. a beading brow
endures humid hours of light;
enjoying the errant, welcomed breeze
hoping twilight brings relief.

FIRST KISS

First Kiss-
first burst of passion
in young love
so eagerly anticipated.
A boy, a girl,
a quiet moment together;
lips meet tentatively
while stars collide.
A tenderness
supplanted by their elders
before lust arrives
to turn the tender tawdry.
An embrace,
awkward, shy, impulsive,
full of meaning,
remembered above all others.
First Kiss,
magical romantic-
tender buds
about to come full bloom.

A LAPSE IN PASSION

Perhaps we've stood too far apart
preparing to embrace;
knowing every line, each crease
etched in each others face.
Perhaps we are too comfortable,
a distance between arms,
when there's a lapse of passion
we must appreciate each others charms.
Perhaps my hand is soft to hold
during one, short kiss
to show we have afections
while there is a dirth of bliss.
Perhaps we've found a gentler way
of showing that we care.
When there's a lapse of passion
we know a fire still burns there.

THROUGH YOUR EYES

I live vicariously through you . . .
the places you've been, the people you know,
the interesting things you do.
I've crossed the scorching sands
upon your camels back
with my imagination.
(alas, it's funds I lack)
As you fly across the oceans,
I sit in the next seat;
ready for adventures,
dangerous, yet, sweet.
I've watched sunsets on horizons
and I've seen the bluest skies.
It's grand to tour this lovely world
if only through your eyes.

THE LABATTES BLUES

He's sitting at the bar tonight
in his best tennis shoes;
in cut offs and a tee-shirt-
He's got the LaBattes Blues.
He's lost in conversation
about all the local views.
He's depressed, he's lonely.
He's got the LaBattes Blues.
The ladies are rejecting him, in ones, then in twos.
He will leave, alone, tonight.
He's got the LaBattes Blues.
He really is a nice guy.
He's just hidden all the clues.
He buys a round for everyone.
He's got the La Battes Blues.
He's sitting at the bar tonight.
It is the life so many choose.
Lost, alone and getting drunk.
He's got the LaBattes Blues.

AN AUGUST VIEW

On this Ohio day,
the sky crackles with
electricity.
August afternoon,
so hot
smells of melting asphalt
meld with lavender,
evergreen and freshly clipped lawns.
A viscous haze envelopes
the aggressive sun;
searing passersby with a muted fire.
Grasses ache for teasing rains,
flirting with thirsting gardens.
Stillness of an absent breeze
lingers in the heat.
Beyond complaints of brackish sweat,
splinters of December cold
buffet harried pedestrians
who forget, too soon,
their summers.

UNDER ACHEIVER

He's more than just a husband, dad;

he's a good man,
shouldering more burdens
than any titan can.
His tasks, difficult so varied.
His ambition at its peak.
He'll never be appreciated
for accolades some seek.
Minutes flow to hours
eddying to days;
filling weeks to months, his years
tempered with the ways
all adults aspire to,
acheive, then carry on,
bouyed by recognition
of battles he has won.

TO OWEN

Light follows his sweet toddlers smile.
The room illuminates about,
glowing, shining all the while
obliterating doubt
that there was ever any boy
who, through no fault of his own
filled so many with such joy,
we can't picture him as grown.
Even when he's bad(not he!)
and given child-like whim,
our world is as it should be
just because of him.

MY HEAVEN

If the world would end tomorrow,
my life would not change.
It has been filled with precious days
I never would exchange.
Not for riches nor accolades,
my pride is not so grand
that I'd fail to appreciate
the blessings at my hand.
If the world would end tomorrow,
I'd put the kids to bed
and let the troubles of my kind
drift out of my head.
It has been a joyful ride,
full of love and bliss.
If the world would end tomorrow,
my heaven would be this.

HE'LL ALWAYS BE MY BABY

He'll always be my baby
even when he's lined with age,
when every step he takes is slow
and his mind will not engage.
He'll always be my baby,
even when he's old and gray,
when there's no tooth left in his head,
he'll not have aged a day.
The weariness of our lives drag on.
All living things grow old.
I'll still want to protect him
to keep him safely from the cold.
He's a man, now, with a family.
His days, I hope, are full of joy.
No matter where life takes him,
he's still my baby boy.

OUT OF BONDAGE

Today's the day I was set free;
turned lose of shackles
I never knew I had.
In the space of an hour,
my chains fell away-
who knew I'd be so sad.
He was happy as he left,
said "see ya"
to go fishing with his dad.
The rain fell in fury, like tears
I would finally cry.
Ther's no relief to lose a love
even when they die.
We should have been united.
In our grief, our strengths belie.
We never held each other or
had the guts to try.
I was so lost, confused, so rootless-
a ship, adrift at sea.
I never would admit to them
just what he meant to me.
I could not acknowledge
what their loss might be.
The pieces of my shattered heart
were all that I could see.
He has been gone these many years.
I have moved on in life . . .
a mother four times over,
somebody elses wife.
In some unselfish way he loosed me
to reach, to stretch through strife.
Our broken dreams are prisons
that bind us all to life.

I'M SORRY

I never accepted her terrible pain;
her loss, her disbelief
could be as great or greater
than my own selfish grief.
I could only see my loss,
subtract two people from my life.
I couldn't grasp she'd ceased to be
his mother and his wife.
I could say I lost them, too-
my sorrow just as great
as one whose husband and whose son
had exited her life.
It is too late
to say "I love you" or "Good-bye"
We should have been there for each other.
I now share her position
as a wife and as a mother.
I owe her my apologies.
I could have been more kind
but the words "I'm Sorry"
are the only ones I find.

NG

I kissed you,
your life ebbing into my disheartened soul.
You came back to me at th end of your life.
I tried to comfort you by comforting myself.
A love, so deep, in our souls
that others could not comprehend.
through my most trying hours,
you were there for me.
I could tell you anything.
They tried to take you from me
but you always come back to me in dreams-
part of me forever.
We won.
Our love, our devotion spans time and space.
And I know, you remember me
as I remember you.

BURY MY HEART AT WOUNDED KNEE

Weep not for what will never be
on lands devoid of grass, of tree;
but dust as far as eyes can see

bury my heart at wounded knee

when one man is no longer free
his honor is the last to flee,
bravely standing for you, for me

bury my heart at wounded knee

Aware of suffering peoples, we,
the crow, blackfoot, the noble cree
traverse our eternity

bury my heart at wounded knee

the journey never ends, you see,
as long as feet do not fall free
to walk this path of destiny

bury my heart at wounded knee

look passed the horizon to that lone tree
open your heart, now, truly see
what peaceful people still can be

bury my heart at wounded knee

My time approaches, now I see,
to maintain my dignity
I'll reap what has been sewn for me
Bury nyheart at wounded knee.

UPON WAKING

When I woke up this morning
there was electricity in the air.
Winds buffetted clouds
in a dove gray sky
aching to release rains
held throughout summer.

TO A NEW FRIEND OF NICKS

At last accolades came.
He would leave his mark on the univwerse,
no longer prey to nebulous depression
or feelings of dispair;
hope eclipsed the deathly pall
that was his life.
Recognized for a positive,
proof of his having been would
not be a splatter of blood upon the wall.

NEW MOON. NO MOON

A creature of the night,
I exist on a deep plane of darkness.
Evening embraces my shivering soul
when no veil of stars adorn the sky.
Cloudless, infinite space above me,
covers sleep in a chilled blanket of unrest.
The almanac states 'New Moon'
in absentia,
no proof of this orb is a contradiction.

MY TREASURE

Chloe's smile is honey cream, cherry sweet;
accented by lapis eyes, sable lashes, strawberry locks . . .
When joy illuminates her face,
the world takes a glow,
so surreal, hypnotic.
Such a tiny child,
so pure-a soul of innocent joy.
My heart is held for ransom
when she is out of sight.
I am a prisoner of her charm-
child of my child,
my treasure.

DAY BEGINS

At the beginning of the day
the world wakes,
stretching green arms to the sun.
Morning birds sing, celebrating life.
Children tug at their mothers skirts,
eager to play in the fresh air.
Sun streaks through windows,
cascading over lolling cats
on the sill.
A fresh start, a new beginning,
a chance to right all wrongs and be set free.

SEPTEMBER LAKE

Lake Erie breathes dark and dangerous.
Slate-gray waters merge with near-onyx skies.
Storms threaten the horizon as thunder rumbles.
There is a solemn stillness
embracing the dark as gulls wheel overhead.
Steel clouds engorged with rains
await release.
Jagged streams of light
fracture deepening heavens,
giving way to relief.

LAKE ERIE

She breathe deep into watery swells
exhaling foam and grief.
Petulent, dangerous, whimsical
in her give and take.
From whispering calm to rage,
she beats the quaking sands with an open hand.
No man can know, no sailor can question her reasoning.
She is the mystery that tempts man to tarry
upon her waves,
gathering bounty in boats, buckets . . .
The lady cannot be conquered
or calmed when turbulent moods beset . . .
only weathered by time and disposition.

NO OLD BONES

These two will not create old bones,
hobbled by their name,
by squandered fortunes Heaven owns
to bind them both in shame.

The death of father early on
could not preclude their fate.
The stable life was lost to them
as true love came too late.

So loved, so cherished ;lost in pride-
selfish hearts were not contrite-
They've journeyed through Hell,
side-by-side,
In darkness they unite.

Picked clean, skeletons will clatter
upon the closet floor.
Unaware what was the matter,
they're lost forever more.

Bone by bone articulates,
devoid of flesh's device.
Destiny none capitulates,
sold at a beggers price.

Remnants of a life precludes
all but unhappy ends
as unrequited lives conclude
predestined recommends.

They never reach for steady hands.
They'd rock, they'd cry, they'd moan
caving into her demands,
fate finds them left alone.

These two will not create old bones,
ensnared in history
to jig to their own rattling tones,
eager to dance free.

They will not, I fear, grow to be old.
They'll come unto earth young,
to rest so deeply in the cold
with all youths songs unsung.

SERRATED AND DULL

She would leave her mark on life
(three times mother, likewise, wife)
chords severed by a rusty knife-
serrated and dull.

She would cut a swath passed years
(where no one dried her futile tears)
all blades are not as one appears-
serrated and dull.

She would trim a heavy pelt
(unaware how others felt)
green eyes caused tempered steel to melt-
serrated and dull.

She would eclipse the breaking sun
(sabres poised to fight as one)
cocealed her points until she's done-
serrated and dull.

She would win while others lose
(all weapons her own to choose)
to leave them, bloodied in their shoes-
serrated and dull.

GOOD SPORTS

We get along,
our talents differing,
our excellence un matched
by each others aspect.

You know nothing
of meter, rhyme;
while I am ignorant
of periods, quarters, rules . . .

Our games differ
in some uniform degree,
never calling sides
nor suffering defeat.

Being good sports,
we do not keep score.
We two commit to gameplans
until the whistle blows.

QUITE UNKNOWN TO ME

I knew nothing of your idioms,
cobbled together in realities
quite unknown to me.

You knew nothing of my struggles,
fighting to survive the tumult of being
quite unknown to me.

I knew nothing of your artiface,
finely wraught by fire, steel
quite unknown to me.

You knew nothing of my brevity,
punctuated by forever
quite unknown to me.

SHARED MEMORIES

We shared memories,
mother and I.
I amazed her with my recall.
She corrected my mis-remembering.

One event remembered differently
from a smaller perspective,
seen from further down-
a childs vantage point.

I sensed a lack, a discontent.
The mother, over-burdened, harried-
frustration for us both.
She gave up. I went along, agreeable.

I wanted my mother,
she wanted safety, security
for me, for her future,
for her other children.

We loved each other in despairation.
We suffered loss of self,
of each other.
I remembered, somewhere, I was loved.

I sensed, once, that I was valued
before the parade of brothers
and of the death
of one more fair than I.

OLD LOVERS

Old lovers,
do not be remiss
do not ignore,
do not dismiss
the all important cuddle, kiss.
Tide and time may turn.

Old lovers,
do not be remiss
when nights drag on'
as long as this.
Romance, sentiments amiss.
It is a loss we yearn.

Old lovers,
do not be remiss
to stoke the fire,
attend the kiss
as flames ebb low,
as embers hiss
somewhere the fires burn.

Old lovers,
do not be remiss
of white hot ardours
one might miss
between the folds of overt bliss
forever promising return.

THE ULTIMATE COST

All must be held accountable
for wrongs they may have done.

There are tributes to be paid
for every battle won.

No one escapes life blemish free.
Deeds levy scars upon each soul.

Only balanced give and take
will render victims whole.

Untold evils hide behind
the most attractive face.

No manner of good deeds done
cause marks to erase.

For myriad of sorrows forced,
for all who suffer, live

asking for forgiveness
which is hardly ours to give.

YOUTH IS WASTED ON THE YOUNG

Now as age eclipses life,
while I have tunes unsung,
I regret my options left to chance.
Youth is wasted on the young.

Energies have come full circle.
The pendulum has swung.
I retrace an ardous trail.
Youth is wasted on the young.

Had I but rememberances,
(chance is cast to worlds far-flung)
I might know my heritage.
Youth is wasted on the young.

My deepest wishes cast upon
the poisons of my tongue.
Might I have weighed my words more carefully.
Youth is wasted on the young.

I relax my hold, now, I let loose
each illusion I have clung.
Realities are for the sure.
Youth is wasted on the young.

Do harken to the winds of change,
to such melodies we've sung.
I must be grateful for what's mine.
Youth is wasted by the young.

The past is but our lives debris,
gold amassed in heaps of dung.
We salvage what is left to us.
Youth is wasted on the young.

THIS CHILD OF MINE

Could it pass, this child of mine,
now, forelorn woman grown,
will reap such an angry harvest
from bitter seeds she's sewn.

Could it pass, this child of mine
will cede all battles fought,
bequeathe whatever gods may be
each vexing answer sought.

Could it pass, this child of mine,
so treasured all her days
will slip my grasp, fade finally,
lost in dark delays.

Could it pass, this child of mine,
will succumb, wull pass away
to only be revealed to those
who share a better day.

Could it pass, this child of mine,
will be stripped from my arms,
only returning to my heart
with her unearthly charms.

Could it pass, this child of mine,
will finally be whole,
will come to know eternity
will heal her fractured soul.

Could it pass, this child of mine,
so fragile, fine as glass;
shattering at daybreak
where broken dreams may pass.

IT IS JULY

The heat is on.
It is July.
We gripe,
we can complain
that we don't know
why we should suffer so
when days are so very hot.
Summer may be many things
but chilling it is not.
Sweat rolls down
the backs of necks
collecting in our creases.
We steam, we bake;we cook, we fry
as temperature increases.
The heat is on.
It is July.
The heat is here to stay.
Our only true concession
is to wait another day.
It is July.
It is so hot.
The water parks will win
when we cool our heels and other parts
as soon as we get in.

SUMMER HEAT

A brilliant sun ignites the day,
a fire in the heavens.
Heat envelopes the weary.
No promise of rain in a hazy sky
as temperatures, humidity
lingers about our heads.
A heavy layer of air rests above us.
We look past tree tops
praying for rain that never comes.
No clouds mar the constant sky.
Craned necks, narrow eyes see
that brilliant sun is not a bad thing.
We must recall December
when July wears us down with heat.
As all things of man and nature,
this, too, shall pass, repeat.

VANITY

I glanced into the bathroom glass
and much to my surprise
a horrid face had come to pass
before my bleary eyes.
She was a weary, sullen hag
whose countenance is grim,
looking like something a cat would drag
or what might follow him.
A wrinkled brow of weathered skin
where every line and crease
captures light and takes it in
until thoughts of youth soon cease.
I can't believe I look my age.
There must be some mistake.
My advice should all be sage,
so listen for my sake.
I once was young and daring
now my courage has decreased.
I mark my time for caring
with the hope I'll be released.

ACROSS THE BRIDGE

There is a bridge that we must cross
at some point in our lives.
Spanning a short distance,
it will help us arrive at our ultimate destination.
Patches of green edge each end.
Cool waters flow beneath the stone arch,
rippling, calming.
Each rill composes a melody.
The happy brook speaks to us
of possibilities,
evoking scenarios of bliss.
Each step we take toward the other side
moves us closer to our goal.
tried confidently.
Pay attention to the path.
Travel with faith and knowledge
of what awaits across the bridge.

TO THE BEACH

They gather at the lake today
to cool minds, souls;
to chase away oppresing heat
that nature now controls.
Ecru sands blister sandled feet
on the long walk to the water.
Blankets, towels and coolers
dot the searing beach
as bathers gather head to head,
relief within their reach.
Irridescent particles cling to exposed arms, to legs,
rinsed away as rolling waves
offer up debris.
Ice chests melt today
with sodas, beer still cold.
The pulsing shoreline offers all-
warm memories to hold.

WELL-READ

A chapter closes on life today.
The book, well-read, dog-eared,
with favorite passages underlined
for emphasis.
Kept close by, the tome is at hand
so we may thumb through
best-loved pages,
finding inspiration in familiar words.
Oft read volumes need not be shelved
but may be enjoyed again and again-
so the story continues.
Stroke the grainy cover,
riffle pages and remember when the tale was new,
untested.
It is a complete collection of images
of ideas shared by someone who cared.
It is their story. It is our story.
We live life by th ebook.

COME BACK TO OHIO

I understand you must move on.
Far horizons beckon.
New beginnings lure you away from Ohio.
You leave the lake, green, rolling fields,
people who will miss you.
Envy lurks inside out
directed to new people in your life.
I know you will not forget the hearts,
the minds, the lives you've touched
by your kind, gentle methods.
I will miss our easy conversations,
our reliable friendship.
Time will heal the rift of your leaving
with the hope that Floridas perfect sun
will wear on you,
sending you back to Ohio.

ALL ABOARD

Adventures loom ahead.
The boy inside the man has itchy feet.
His palms prickle.
His eyes light with excitement.
The youth has packed away his fairest treasure in his favorite box.
He will leave nothing behind
to retrace his eager steps.
His traveling clothes are laid out,
ready for the journey.
The man may have little fears,'
kniggling doubts of the unknown
but, oh! the boy inside is eversure.
So confident he can barely bide his time
until departure.
It will be a grand explore
for both boy and man.
Their ticket will be punched
as they climb aboard their dream ship
to the brightest future.

NO FAULT OF THEIR OWN

We see the child
as sum and part of us.
Yet, there is something more-
a God-imbued quality
uniquely his own.
How he learns,
how he perceives life around him
is not through our eyes, our senses,
but, something more intimate.
The child comes, an innocent,
uncorrupted but not uncorruptable.
We hold the balast to sway personality.
What we say, how we react,
are learning tools.
We teach the soft, the yielding to conform.
WE must use restraint as we involve
our young to take our world as is;
to understand why they are to be held
accountable for their response
to rules not their own.

OH, LADIES, WILL YOU DANCE?

The fires burn bright, the music's full,
the room's awash with glee.
So, take my hand. Oh, will you dance?
Ladies, will you dance ?
Ladies, will you dance with me?
Oh, hear the lute, the violin, the choirs
now, sing free.
Listen to the music, lass.
Oh, will you dance with me?
Ladies, will you dance with me?
Squires humble, lords ordain;
tables full, the wine flows free.
The earls, the dukes, the courtiers say
"Will you dance with me?
Ladies, will you dance with me?"
The king is hunting in the wood,
a carefree spirit, he.
When he returns, the passion burns.
Oh, will you dance with me?
Ladies, will you dance with me?
Now, time has ebbed too low to flow,
too choked to rush so free.
The lords and king sit still but say
"Will you dance with me?
Ladies, will you dance with me?"
The court is ready to pass on.
Younger men decree;
while old men sit and glower
all youth cries
"Will you dance with me?
Ladies, will you dance with me?"
Young and old unite and they
pass on to some degree.
Neither has the strength, the will
to say" Will you dance with me?
Ladies, will you dance with me?"

FRIENDS/FAMILY

We cannot choose our family;
our friends are less constrained.
We secure allegencies
for any bonds maintained.
Our family is DNA,
biology and fact.
Our friends belong by word, by deed,
by substance and by act.
Our friends appear at any time;
they're in a state of flux.
Our family, fixed, pre-ordained,
ours because of luck.

We can be close to persons
not born of family trees
but rest amid the branches
of connections such as these.

We know a smile, a hug, a look;
we rest in an embrace
of all closest friends we have
when family can't replace.
We are a group, we are a team
gathered for a game.
If done right, friends and family are loved
by us, just the same.

As Night Begins For Me

(as inspired by Elandra)

Now I lay me down to sleep
let all the angels 'round me weep
for all the terrors that I keep
as night begins for me.
Tears and anguish render sleep
void of any good to reap
from sullen poisons as they seep
as night begins for me.
Monsters, devils, demons creep
from some sonombulent so deep
that no angels try to leap
as night begins for me.
Now I lay me down to sleep,
lost in dreams so very deep
that all my secrets I my keep
as night begins for me.
Now I lay me down to sleep,
I pray the Lord my soul to keep
for all my dreams that I may reap
as night begins for me.

THE STOW AWAY

In your hip pocket as you travel,
I have trekked vicariously
to all points of the world.
Through your eyes, such sights beheld
I've seen the wonders
of lands known to my dreams.
I've followed you up mountain trail,
flown across the seas,
always along for the ride.
My passport in my wanderers heart
while customs have no care.
My journies know no boundries.
I've never had to leave my home
to share a trip so fine.
I've envisioned every far-off place
as if these adventures were my own.

MY CONSTANT MOON

In deepest shadow
on dreamless night
you are just a glance away
suspended from illusion-
My constant moon.

Through summer storms
or winters howl
you illuminate my darkest side
secure in my beliefs-
My constant moon.

When chill exceeds
the blankets warmth
you cover me in light
spreading illumination-
My constant moon.

Throughout changes in
the deep blue, in me,
you remain as always known,
brilliant and elusive-
My constant moon.

PRIMA BALLERINA

Elevated to a place of worship,
high upon a pedestal,
she had taken many liberties.

On point, toes bruised, bloodied,
she dances around the truth.
Her circumstance requires
a quicker step,
a demanding choreography.

At dizzying height, she spins out of control,
always the consumate performer.

When her diva days are over,
she will be relegated to the chorus.

No longer in the spotlight,
a pirrouette, exiting the center of attention.
She must return to the real world
where curtain calls are brief.

With tattered toe shoes
hanging from ragged ribbons
before a dimmly lit mirror,
she realizes the dance is over.

LIVE

Take two steps in any direction.
The next right move
may set into motion
events causing change.

No longer running in place,
marking time.
Changes in perspectives, fresh ideas;
motivation brings action.
Action urges progress.

Unless we make a move,
we stand still,
allowing the world to step around us.
Join the dance!

Hear the rythm of you own heart
beating in time with the universe.
Inhale. Exhale. Live!

THE LITTLE GIRL, THE LITTLE BOY

A china doll, left on the floor,
pretty, fragile, easy to ignore.
The little girl, the little boy
have both lost interest
in their favorite toy.

Next to the doll, a teddy bear
whose fur is nappy, threadbare
from much loving.

The little girl, the little boy
forget the toys that brought them
every joy.

Upon a shelf, a carrousell
brightly painted,
stories to tell.
The little girl, the little boy
playing their tune to annoy.

When toys are new
we pay the price
the toys played with once or twice.
The little girls, the little boy
too soon outgrow a favorite toy.

A china doll, a teddy bear
frogotten as if they were never there.
The little girl, the little boy
have found new diversions to employ.

A stack of toys, broken apart
no longer mending a broken heart.
The little girl, the little boy
have outgrown their need
for any shiny toy.

LAST SNOW

Outside my window
soft, tufted branches move
so slightly.

Barely a breeze
to lift slight limbs
into the air.

Drifting snows
blanket every open space
in purest white.

Too soon pristine cover
turns to urging mire
bidding flowers come.

WE PRAY

We pray
down on our knees in supplication
to a man
a good man who lived once
who suffered at mans hand.

We pray
because we're told we should bow
down to God
a God who is at once vengeful and forgiving.

We pray
hoping fates turn, that good will
follow
humbled by an ideal.

We pray
pretending that something larger
than ourselves
will bestow wisdom, bring good fortune
if we do things by the book.

OH, GOD

Oh, God,
do you hear me cry
anguished in the night?
Do you listen to my pleas
or just ignore
the damaged in your sight?

Oh, God,
are we your children
meant to suffer at your hand?
Are we made lesser souls
denied a chance to stand?

Oh, God,
are we created in your image
to be given feet of clay?
Are we molded true to form by you
while headed for the day?

Oh, God,
must we all kneel down,
surrender to ideals?
Must we give up humility
to a counterfeit that feels?

Oh, God,
are we expected
to reach the mountain top?
Are we allowed to live out lives
before you order 'stop'?

BLESSED I

I save my tears, like treasure,
in a box made for such jewels.
Safe keeping for the memories,
the sadnesses of fools.

I spent my dreams, each dollar
from an account that's overdrawn;
to wake from sleeps tormented state
hours before the dawn.

I collect my thoughts in increments
in meter, thought and rhyme;
to tell a tale of polished truths
that tarnish after time.

I know my many motives
to garner treasures dear,
to grow stronger in my love of life
until I feel no fear.

I keep a promise to myself
made under duress
to capture love deep in my soul.
I am my own to bless.

WE ARE MERELY MORTALS

We are merely mortals,
full of lifes regrets,
known for all our failings,
for all our unpaid debts.

We are merely mortals
whose lives have passed us by,
leaving us to wonder how
we can live until we die.

We are merely mortals
acting out a play,
reading lines, reciting
words we've learned along the way.

We are merely mortals
meant to play our part
upon a dimly lighted stage
to suffer for our art.

We are merely mortals
with so very much to give,
gathering the promises
allowing us to live.

THE SECRET

My friend told me a secret
She said "There is no God."
I asked her where we came from.
She looked at me, quite odd.
"We came from dust eons ago.
We are but air and dirt."
Open to new ideas,
I thought "how could it hurt?"
We all believe in something
whether God or primordial ooze.
Life was started somewhere.
The what is ours to choose.

WE MEET SO MANY PEOPLE

We meet so many people
as our lives progress.
If we really get to know them
is anybody's guess.

We meet so many people
on a sunny afternoon
yet, only know them dimly,
by the scant light of the moon.

We meet so many people
cleave some close to our breast
selected, chosen blindly
to love above the rest.

We meet so many people
by choice we will be loyal,
call many friend, some enemy
before we shed this mortal coil.

I MISS MY UNCLE BILL

I was once known as the pet
of a childhood I would soon regret
every pattern that was set
by my Uncle Bill.

Now I sinned by practice yet
for years I've suffered to forget
I've whined, I've worried, How I'd fret.
I'd angered Uncle Bill.

I've committed some great sin.
I stood my ground,
but did I win?
I don't know where I could begin
to apologize to Bill.

I fear my family's lot is cast
as I have known them from the past.
It is in death I'll see them last.
I miss my Uncle Bill.

FRUSTRATED TEARS

When waking, sleep grow closes these days,
any actions not required
are subject to a few delays
when love is less desired.

I know of women in my place
who might hesitste to stay
as rest eclipses waking
and he sleeps his life away.

Throughout the years we've sacrificed
we both have given much.
So quitting does not factor in
when we recall familiar touch.

His tender hands on afternoons
when romantic scenes reveal
the solid, firm foundation
lack of desires conceal.

So I must mold, I must adapt
I must be ready to engage
when my husband, lover, dearest friend
falls prey to crushing age.

When passions fade to holding hands
and sex sadly disappears,
we must adjust to new demands,
hold back frustrations tears.

THE GIFT

I have had a nodding aquaintence with madness.
I defy modern decree
to be swallowed by the sadness
that insists on chasing me.

I have flirted with insane ideals
when I have been depressed.
I have survived the sad appeals
when I've been death obsessed.

I have succumbed to torments hand
when the punishments were mine.
I struggled free of grim demand
when fact and fallacy combine.

I have been downto the bottom rung
where I stared from the abyss.
I turned my head from words that stung
to avoid the demons kiss.

I have traveled to the depths of Hell
where all other souls find rest.
I shout until God hears me yell,
begging to be blessed.

I found fate was but a sudden rift
where my dreams could offer bliss,
when I accepted madness as a gift
I knew I'd survive like this.

MY FUTURE WAITS

I find myself upon a trail,
a quest of my own making.
I refuse to let my venture fail
by hesitation, by forsaking
the powers of my mind
where fearless seeds are planted
and left for me to find.
Now I will not embrace the dark of death
once found within my soul.
I demand the rythm of my breath
for I will be made whole.
I am the mistress of my fate.
I will have what I ask and more.
I feel I am deserving of
what my future has in store.

SPIRIT VS RELIGION

The dogma of religion is
confused with Spiritual course.
However, spiritual leanings
prevail upon a force
that is always kind, is loving,
is just to one and all.
The dogma of religion
responds to a darker call.
Those who follow spirit are,
each one, made whole
embracing truth, hold, faith
as precepted of the soul.
The dogma of religion
relieves upon the guilty heart,
procuring insecurities
to break egos apart.
A spirit filled dominion lasts
through mysteries and doubt
supporting all who will believe
that goodness will win out.
The dogma of religion holds
the sword above bowed heads
weaving tails of torment, fear
with greedy little threads.
The spiritual have no need of threats,
just promisies,
the give and take combine
to show avenues the spirit takes
to arrive at the devine.

ALAS, OLD LOVERS

Alas, old lovers
gone long from me
by time, by space by breath;
alas old lovers
gone long from me
surrendering to death.
Alas, old lovers, gone long from me
embers rendered cold;
alas, old lovers gone long from me,
never to grow old.
Alas, old lovers
gone long from me,
old images of lust;
alas, old lovers
gone long from me,
your destiny is dust.
Alas, old lovers,
gone long from me
when passions could hold sway;
alas, old lovers,
gone long from me,
our youth has blown away.
Alas, old lovers,
gone long from me,
our love, our dreams go on;
Alas old lovers,
gone long from me,
you're never really gone.

THE KING AND QUEEN OF DISCO

We met in smoke, in secrecy
each played a different role.
The King and Queen of disco
each an ill-fated soul.

We clutched at passions remnants.
We sacrificed control.
The king and queen of disco
needed to feel whole.

We devoured the velvet night.
We danced the night away.
the king and queen of disco-
we're strangers in the day.

We held tightly to romantic scraps
mistaking sex for bliss.
The king and queen of disco,
swallowed by a kiss.

We faked our way to self-esteem,
devoured each image cast-
the king and queen of disco
have found their place at last.

ALL THAT I NEED NOW

We shared our flesh.
You won my heart
on the stage that was your life.
I played the smallest part.

We met in heat,
succumbed by flame;
when morning yawned
I had to ask your name.

We danced, we drank;
you preached to me
of all the roles I'd play,
what I should be.

We lived a lie,
we split the truth
of our wasted effort of all our wasted youth.

We ran from love
embraced the spark
of all our passoind spent
there within the dark.

We two lost touch;
I hear you'd died.
I cannot cry for you
as I once cried.

We'll meet again,
if the fates allow,
I have memories,
that's all that I need now.

HE LIVES ON (TO SKIP)

Her tears fill a great, golden chalice.
he holds it fast to his lips.
She greedily draws her sorrows
between her quivering lips.

Her dreams are kept safe in a casket-
a box of fine gems and gold.
She takes them out nightly to keep them
in a memory to fractured to hold.

Her life is used up, it is wasted,
on a man who cares not for her sake.
Yet, she goes to him often in moonlight
encouraged by love that they make.

Her joys are all subject to passions
that her secrets, her wishes have lent.
She can never recoup all her losses
of moments wasted in love she has spent.

Her days will go on here without him;
he died young and now, he is gone.
She has beautiful pictures in memory,
in deepest regret, he lives on.

OH, MY LOVE, MY HUSBAND

Oh, my love, my husband, my life
many lovers breathed before
yet, I have sequestered them to dust
because I love you more.

Oh, my love, my husband, my life,
I have loved other men;
I have discovered at your side
how to love again.

Oh, my love, my husband, my life,
there are sad seeds I've sewn.
yet, you have chosen me, your wife,
by grace, by love, your own.

TONIGHT MY HUSBAND
AS LONG AGO

Tonight, my husband of long ago-
children of our child rest-
A part from you I cleave to them
in my grandmothers heart.

Tonight my husband of long ago,
these children grow so tall;
I'll try to tell good tales of you
From scant memories, that's all.

Tonight, my husband of long ago,
another takes your place-
he carries your mantle deftly, still,
each child bears your face.

Tonight, my husband of long ago,
I see in each small child
every hurt forgiven
in a life now reconciled.

Tonight, my husband, of long ago,
though I recall your touch,
only these striplings in my care
bring my heart so much . . .

Tonight, my husband of so long ago,
though our union has passed,
our children and each child of theirs
is the eternal bond that lasts.

THE MAN I CALL MY OWN

A good man came into my life
who deemed me fit to be his wife,
has borne me through travails and strife-
this man I call my own.

A good man who took me to his side
who chose me to be his legal bride;
knew I could be faithful and abide-
this man I call my own.

A good man who saw me as I was
who championed my lost cause
wrencthed me from distrasters claws-
this man I call my own.

A good man I took to my bed
who chose to love my chance instead-
to look beyond, to see ahead,
this man I call my own.

A good man I have come to know
has met my demons blow-flow-blow
and has my eternal love to show,
this man I call my own.

OH, BEAUTY, DREAM

Oh, beauty, dream
please, do not take
your magic from the night.
If not for sleeps unconscienceness
my souls sanity's at stake.

Oh, beauty, dream,
please, do not take
your vision from my sight.
If not for sleeps deft imagery,
my madness memories make.

Oh, beauty, dream please, do not take
your answers to my plight.
If not for all the twists, the turns,
realities are fake.

Oh, beauty, dreams,
please, do not take
your fragile truth, your night.
If not for the simple strength of dreams,
my thoughts would not foresake.

Oh, beauty, dream
please, do not take
your precious rest to make it right.
If not for slumbers casualties
my voracious psyches slake.

Oh, beauty, dream
please, do not take
your tender, endless sight
to leave me blind, leave me alone
with thoughts just for my sake.

OUR DREAMS

Our dreams, our nightmares take us
to a distant realm
with a stalwart captain who's quite mad
standing a the helm.

Our dreams, our nightmares take us
far beyond the stars
where mere mortals can appreciate
their banal waking hours.

Our dreams, our nightmares take us
where vessels do not transport,
to a place of abstract beauty
of the must fantastic sort.

Our dreams, our nightmares take us
while all the wakeful rant
of everywhere they wish to go
yet, if not for sleep, they can't.

Our dreams, our nightmares take us
beyond facts we don't believe,
to visions open eyes, be blind
only the dreamers sights conceive.

THE ANNOITED

For those who feel they do no wrong,
for those who know their rightful place;
for those who never give an inch,
for those who must save face.

For the fey, the sanctimonious,
for the godly man, the wife;
for the pundants, for the prophets, too,
for those afraid of life.

For those whose dreams are put on hold,
for all who won't believe;
for every hopeless, lonely soul,
for ideas men conceive.

For every mis-step on the road,
for each untraveled path;
for every fabled wayfarer,
for dangers aftermath.

For every hope extinguished,
for every quashed desire;
for every smile that never was,
for every smoldering fire.

I hope someday to show these wounded,
who've been damaged by such strife,
that there is a way revealing
the happy, joyful life.

I, I AM

I am not of the annoited
who stare from the crevass
at all godly endeavors
who, gladly, take a pass.

I watch them as they pod along
within their busy day,
ever careful, following blindly
leading to delay.

I am not of the annoited
who often question "why?"
man must work so hard each day
while, all they know will die.

I am not of the annoited
whose answers are so pat,
they stomp around in circles
never knowing where they're at.

I watch the weary workers
as they struggle, toil;
as they endeavor to hold on to
their weighty, earthly coil.

I am not of the annointed
for I wasted much of youth.
Yet, somehow, I have reached a place
where I know my own truth.

DEAR MARGE, DEAR NICOLE

Tonight is the night our lives changed forever.
Almost the exact time I am writing this.
Ma called.
"Don't be upset" she said.
"There's been an accident"
I tried not to think much of it.
I knew Ma . . . your son
I washed my hair.
(that always made me feel better)
It started to storm.
I tried to watch T.V.
but it was so late,
they'd been gone for so long . . .
Then, there was a knock at the door.
It was Peter Miller and Benny.
Benny was crying.
I'll never forget the pain in his eyes.
I screamed. I knew they were dead.
Peter took me to your house to tell you
o fthe accident.
You were asleep.
When I knelt to touch your shoulder you screamed
"They're gone! They're gone!"
I got you dressed and we all went down
to Turkey Creek to wait.
Wait for what? I wondered.
For Stan to jump out of the bushes, giggling
or Clarence walking up from the shadows,
cigarette in his lips, smile on his face . . .
the joke on us . . .
or wait for a body to roll out of the gray surf
on to the wet sand.

The coast guard scoured the waters,
their helicopter hovered overhead.
I kept looking up the beach, waiting for Stan to appear.
He never did that night.
You stayed close to Betty and Benny for comfort and I had no one.
That's when the seed was planted.
WE should have been a comfort to each other.
But, we weren't.
Then, when you did try to reach out, I pulled away . . .
too deep in my own grief to see your pain.
You had lost your husband *and your son.*
I loved Clarence, too, and I thought my loss too great to share.
Throughout the search,
we formed our own protective circles.
You tried to cross over but I held you at arms length.
I didn't have to agree with all of your ideas
but I could have negotiated more gently.
If I'd known then what I know now-
the bond of a mothr for her son-
who has a wife who doesn't like her,
who has given her two beautiful grand childern she treasures . . .
If I lost my husband, I would be devasted, inconsolable.
If I lost both, I would be lost.
But, if by losing my son,
it meant losing my beautiful grandchildren,
it would fracture my soul.
I vow not to let the distance between that young woman
and myself grow into a chasm
that cannot be broached.
I will reach out to her, try to be a friend and confidant.
I will be careful in my gift giving
and considerate of her family.

I will try to respect her beliefs and ideas
no matter how different from my own.
I will help her, when asked and be there
when she feels she needs me.
I will let her know the door to my heart is open and she is welcome.
If that had been our experience, it would have been different-
for both of us.
It would have been less painful.
I ran. You pushed.
I balked at your control.
If only we had talked.
It should have been a comfort and a colsulation.
I'll never know the scope of your grief as you could never know mine,
but it has taught me to respect the young woman
my son has chosen as his partner in life.
He loves her and, because I love him,
I hope to grow to love her too.
Afterall, she loves my son-
how bad can she be?

GRANDMA MYERS

I remember Grandma Myers,
when she lived in her chicken coop apartment.
It was cozy, comfortable, with its chemical toilet
and homey outhouse.
I loved Grandmas house.
I felt safe, I felt loved, I felt valued.
Grandma always had her special cookies-poor house annie(scotch
    cookies)
On her table were two cut glass candy dishes-
one with star mints, the other with butterscotch discs.
I would sit on her green plaid futon
while we watched Lawerce Welk.
(I didn't care for Lawrence Welk but I cared for Grandma.)
Minnie Myers would play solitare or she would crochet,
smoking her Phillip Morris Commanders.
There was a yellow tendril of hair escaping
her hair net, colored by the smoke.
Grandma had small feet, like my Brittainy,
ridiculously small.
She had a huge bust.
Her dresses always rode high in the back.
She played poker and chuck-a-luck.
(A skill she passed on to Nick and I)
If a person can be described as a color,
Grandma was a kaliedascope.
She was an array of shades and scents; of flowers and sounds.
Grandma was a modern woman, icon of her time.
I wish my childerncould have known her.
She was a treasure.
Her thoughts, her advice-such wisdom.
Minnie Mae Riley Higgins Fischer Myers-
a woman for all seasons.
My mentor, my idol, my grandma.

A SIT DOWN MEAL

Ma made pies . . .
for the family, for friends;for holidays, for any day.
Her lemon pie, her pumpkin were sought after.
Perfect merigues, crusts to melt in your mouth.
She cooked according to her own style
with a little bit of grandma's flair.
Potatoes at every meal, bread on the table,
everybody sitting down together in the kitchen.
A glass of water, desert . . .
I tried to emulate these rituals with my children;
with Gabe and Izzy and Elandra when they were with me.
We miss so much-
eating in front of the television, on the run . . .
I miss the community of dinner time in my childhood.
It was a structure, a ritual-
Steady, reliable, predictable.
The substanc of a family meal,
whether of dinner or holiday,
to share a meal,
to laugh, to smile, to eat.
To be a unit, a family.

MY GIFT TO THE AGES

My gift tto the ages,
my words, my thoughts, my dreams.
I hope amuse, provoke ideas
in a world that often seems
too difficult to manage,
too sad to carry on.
We anguish, waking, sleeping,
ambivilent toward dawn.
I hope to paint a scenario
where beauty's bless us all;
where colored leaves are treasured
each day before they fall.
Where the bluster of November
eases into holidays,
where everyone's a child at heart
who grows and lives and plays.
I hope to play a melody
where images may bring,
will find us ever hoping
for fertile days of spring.
Where a shoots push up
through muck and mire
from some unwordly power
to grace us with the beauty
of a fragrant April flower;
where sultry breeze embraces us
on less temporate days
to shield us from the brilliance
of suns punishing rays.
I hope to show a side of man,
of woman and of child
embracing all differences
and we are free to reconcile
every wrong done to them,

forgive each sorrow, each cruel ploy
who forgives a foe, who's learned from life
a way to just enjoy
the beauty of a given day
the lyric in a laugh-
I hope my words, my thoughts, my dreams
have cut their pain in half
to perhaps help them acknowledge
we are, each one, the same
no matter whether we're unknown
or a prisoner of fame.
I hope my words, my thoughts, my dreams
that I transcribe upon these pages
will be embraced as a gift to all-
my gift to the ages.

SOMETHING TO REMEMBER YOU BY

When you died,
I gave all your clothes away.
Your side of the closet was bare,
your drawers empty . . .
Believing absence of these scraps
would make me miss you less.
Late one night, I tried to sleep.
I longed for some vestige of you.
I rummaged, tore, searched
throughout the house we shared
for somwthing, anything
that held your scent.
I had been very thorough
being rid of you.

OF LOVE AND GRIT

Frailties of love,
residue found at the bottom of a grid,
shaken, gently,
to separate artifacts from rubble;
re-construed from fragile pieces, edges, jagged,
inscribed by ancient hands
to tell slight stories.
Multitudes sigh of loss,
of heartache, of longing . . .
a ragged breath escapes word of mouth.
Shattered hearts collect
puzzle pieces connected
to form a true image of forgotten love.

ENOUGH, MY GOD, ENOUGH

Do not strip this love from me.
I've been as good as I can be.
Let him go. Punish me.
Enough, my God, enough.
A part of me these many years,
we've cried, we've dried so many tears.
To lose him-the utmost of my fears.
Enough, my God, enough.
We have struggled through so much,
never breaking promises, such.
Do not deprive me of his touch.
Enough, my God, enough.
He is the half that makes me whole
when blighted moments take their toll,
the steadfast warrior for my soul.
Enough, my God, enough.
Oh, my God, I do implore,
I pray you, please, do not ignoe
the blood smeared on our humble door.
Enough, my God, enough.
If you excise him from my life
to cause me widow, no more wife,
I will not succumb to strife.
Enough, my God, enough.
How difficult can it truly be
to offer alms to such as me.
I yearn, not, to be set free.
Enough, my God, enough.
To bind two souls like ours as one,
to saction love to be undone . . .
Must we surrender? Admit you've won?
Enough, my God, enough.

GOLD STAR MOTHERS

We gave America our sons.
We sent them off to war-
to jungles, deserts, combat-
what were they fighting for?
Some came home in coffins,
some wished they had a box
to escape the nightmares
when wartime horror knocks.
The living dead in uniform,
hear 'taps'at each parade,
reliving every battle scene
they stood, they fought, they prayed.
Those who were not killed outright
were crippled in their soul.
No mere patriotism offered
could ever render them whole.
To all the grieving families'
to mothers, near and far,
are reminded of their loss
when they display that star.
Gold star mothers, one and all,
never thought about it twice.
Their sons, willing to fight, to fall
condoned their sacrifice.
Every mother who has lost a son,
within, without the war-
to see them damaged so,
wonder what these boys fought for.
For their loss, the grieving homes,
(all know who they are)
proudly placed in the window pane-
the symbolic golden star.

A scrap od cloth, a little cord,
gold stars hang in window frames.
Neighbors know the boy, the man,
though some don't recognize the names.
There are many victims here,
they know who they are,
united in their pain, their grief.
Tears only mask the scar
of tender boys, well-loved, now lost
whose ashes fill some jar;
whose lifeless corpse was shipped back home
remembering why poor mothers
received that golden star.

THERE WAS A LITTLE GIRL

Once upon a summer day
there was a little girl
who believed she was a princess
when she gave her skirts a twirl.
Once upon a crowded stage
they labled her a star.
There was a little girl
who aimed her sights too far.
There was a little girl
who didn't set her standards high,
settling for bitter dregs,
forever asking 'why?'
There was a little girl,
awash in fames applause,
dazzled those beneath her
who shared a common cause.
There was a little girl
who sat upon a lonely throne,
content to rule a Kingdom
that never was her own.

MY FRIEND FROM FAR AWAY

I got a call the other day.
My friend from far away
told me that she was okay
to keep worry at bay.
At times my mind goes astray,
not hearing what she has to say-
an honored veteran of the fray-
my friend from far away.
A pound of flesh some would assay
to face the issues as they may.
Every favor asked received a 'nay'
My friend from far away.
Some days we're little girls at play
who hopand skip;who swing and sway
as all our problems ebb away,
my friend from far away.

HIS DISOBEDIENT CHILD

On this night, discharged of care,
(I shake my little fist at God)
smuggly in his realm elsewhere
I am
his disobedient child.
One pious heart cannot compare
(I shake my little fist at God)
yet speak amid and thus declare
I am his disobedient child.
Where myth and rumor gnash and tear
(I shake my little fist at God)
to free me lest I embrace dispair
I am
his disobedient child.

I KNOW WHERE I GO

I have no fear, no dread of death
I know where I go.
I walk a clear, a steady path
avoiding many snares.
I travel in humility
as careful as one dares.
I have no fear, no dread of death,
I know where I go.
I walk a clear, a steadfast path
stepping over rills and creeks,
listening to each whisper of my soul
as my conscience speaks.
I have no fear, no dread of death,
I know where I go
This life, this essence, too, will pass
and when my journey's done,
I will find myself again
where I'd once begon.
I have no fear, no dread of death,
I know where I go.

WHEN I'M BROKE

What kind of wine goes with Mac-n-cheese?
You know, Kraft, in a box-I am dressed for four star fare
in my underwear and socks.
A chardonay, a hearty red;
Chablis, a bland rose';
a cabernet, a deep merlot,
something with bouquet.
This brilliant orange
is not quite what most gourmets had in mind-
my menu of wine and cheese
is of the meager kind.
of middle-late night dining when fridge and cupboards bare
of simple appetizers, of interesting fare.
What kind of wine goes with what is left
from some meal of distant past?
To quaff from some chipped coffee cup,
enjoying to the last.
Cheap wine on ice,
a screw on top
in every fruity flavor
accompanying my mac-n-cheese
allowing me to savor
the simple pleasures left to me
when I have less to spend
until next payday blesses
with a heartier blend.

I'M SMART!
(To Elandra)

I'm smart!
If I were beautiful instead,
wore golden tresses on my head,
I might finally get ahead, but
I'm smart!
I keep company with dread
with only dreams to share my bed.
All my youthful hopes have fled. But
I'm smart!
Pretty is as pretty does
and pretty, well, I never was.
I know I'm alone because
I'm smart!
When some cute boy gives me a twirl
I claim I'm not that kind of girl.
My social life is a total swirl. But,
I'm smart!
Getting 'A's" is not enough
when a tween agers life is rough.
I'm neither ditz, nor doll nor puff. But,
I'm Smart!

KING ME

I reign, an impotent ruler
while I bluster and huff.
My subjects rebel,
take me to task.
I cling, selfishly, to my throne.
I struggle with my birthright
in this kingdom of suffering.
The pages of my edict are secret yet unsealed,
legible only to those who understand
words are not free;
only offered to the select.
Truths, hoarded by the greedy,
the comfortable . . .
scraps of paper, mere scribbles . . .
our scriptures quite inadequate
to guide us during this seige called life.

AS THE STARS CATCH FIRE

We met as lovers, long ago,
not knowing where our lives might go.
We waited for the heavens show
as the stars caught fire.
Day-by-day our passions grew
perceived as real by precious few.
Something happened, that we knew
as the stars caught fire.
Day and night, our company,
proved our love was meant to be-
there for all the world to see
as the stars caught fire.
We have had these many years
to battle jealousies and fears,
to laugh out loud, to battle tears
as the stars caught fire.
We've had a life of true romance
to hold each other in the dance,
glad we finally took a chance,
as the stars caught fire.

MID-NOVEMBER OHIO

Bare branches scrape together.
Skeletal arms embrace,
encircling crackling fields.
Brown, biege, ecru
brush rims of creeks, crisp, dry.
Waters move slowly
through russet hills
winding through asphalt.
Expanses pass buildings,
made stark by ravaging winds.
No flower, not a leaf graces bush, tree;
Only blanketing roots to rot in time.
Snapping underfoot,
none can travel quietly throughout.
Deer track men in brushy domain,
staying safe, away.
Pre-winter chill wraps the city with frigid air.
Soon, sprinkles of white will enhance ragged ground.

I'M SORRY, SAYS IT ALL

If I have harmed in any way,
if I have caused a tear to fall,
there are few words to remedy, so,
I'm sorry says it all.
If my words have cut you,
If you, then, hide behind a wall,
it may not make a difference if
I'm sorry says it all.
If my actions speak too loudly,
if my tales seem very tall,
let me make amends because
I'm sorry says it all.
If youre heart, like mine, is broken,
if your days take on a pall,
let me chase the clouds away.
I'm sorry says it all.
If my sincere apology is wasted breath, that's all,
cast my whisperings aside.
I'm sorry says it all.

THREE DAYS GRACE

There are times, embarassed,
when I've fallen on my face
being saved at the last moment
within my three days grace.
There are times I've been too busy
to enjoy a child's embace;
coming to my senses
within my three days grace.
There are hurtful words, once uttered,
apologies cannot erase
unless amends are to be made
within my three days grace.
There are times I've trouble keeping up
with this punishing pace.
I must take a breath, hold on tight
within my three days grace.

WHEN

When my world is roiled in troubles,
when my options are too few.
I listen to that voice inside
that tells me what to do.
When my ego's had a beating,
when it's battered, crushed and bruised,
I call upon on inner strength
so seldom. if ever used.
When my youth has ebbed to middle age,
when self esteem erodes,
I find the path too rocky
so I search for cleaner roads.
When my talents become suspect,
when I cannot see beyond the curve,
I clench my fist, I forge ahead,
I take what I deserve.
When I ride in my crusade
upon a hollow horse;
I travel on in infamy
until Time runs its course.

ALL MY DAYS WERE GOLDEN YEARS

All my days have meaning,
laughter, song or tears.
Love that fills my heart thus far
presents me golden years.
All my days are blessings
to brave, succumb to fears;
Courage, gifts from the heart
presents me golden years.
All my days are treaasures
valued as careers.
Sacrifice pays dividends
presents me golden years.
All of my dreams align ledgers-
some sorely in arrears-
accounts soon to be balanced
presents me golden years.
All of my beloved family
gathers as my end nears.
The love, the grace, the gratitude
presents me golden years.

DAD WAS

Dad was a man of chosen woeds.
If he said somwthing,
he meant it-
a promise, golden;
a rebuke, a curse.
Dad was a man of few words.
If he chose to speak,
we'd listen;
each statment a gem,
affirmations, blessings.
Dad was a man of select words.
If he shared a thought,
he'd open up,
each admonition,
each reproach
attempts to right a wrong.
Dad was a man of weighing words.
if he offered his advice
his encouragement increased
intrinsicly in value.
Dad was a man of wise words.
If syllables were golden,
each offering would gleam
from mines too deep
to stay hidden
from wisdoms reach.

MY NEW YEARS RESOLUTION

My New Years resolution
was never to be wise;
always to capitulate
not fearing compromise.
My New Years resolution-
be deaf to no ones cries;
always perceiving hardship
through the sufferers eyes.
My New Years resolution
was to embrace the lies
that neither harm not help us,
though surely justifies
my New Years resolution.

IF I

If I made a promise,
to dry your every tear,
would you put away your hanky
which you hold so very near
If I break that promise
as you cry yourself to sleep,
would your eyes grow red and swollen,
full of secrets you must keep?
If I keep a secret
that you fear if told
would place you in so tight a spot
you'd be looked upon as bold?
If I tell your secret,
just between us two,
would you question every moment,
if you only knew?
If I let you in on something,
would you ever question why
I'd take you into confidence
when telling you a lie?
If I hid some grand agenda,
would you seek to find a way,
uncovering deception
while advantages delay?
If I cannot keep a secret
if I have promises unkept;
each confidential musing
adds up to tears we've wept.

WHEN NIGHT MEETS DAY

When does late give way to early?
Who guards each dream we save?
When we cannot close our eyes
to the promise darkness gave?
When do we cast out demons
who hammer at our door?
When do we surrender
to the gifts that we ignore?
When do we treasure starlight?
Who does not envy sun
when rising high above our hopes
to beg he is the one?
When can we hope for peaceful nights?
Who cautions days to blend?
when day and night meet face to face
with wakeful days that end?
When do we cut our losses?
Who can live without their sleep
whe dust, decay and broken dreams
to the weary souls who weep?
When does the night seem endless?
Who mixes nights with day
when nightmares speak to visions threat
to never go away?

I'M GLAD TO NOT BE THERE

I'm lost in Tudor England
in the days of kings and queens;
of jousting and beheading
and the intrigues in between.
I recognize dear Henry
as an image of a man
who was too far corrupted
justifying all he can.
I feel so for Queen Katheryn,
so far away from Spain;
that she was left alone to ache
in loneliness and pain.
I ache for fateless Anne Boelyn
when the crown severed her head.
She never had the chance to live
before they left her dead.
I wonder how such a strong king
could unsuccessfully wed
and blame his many mistresses
for the problems of his bed?

THE SOFT PLACE

I'll be that one place,
the soft palce where you land,
when accomplishments
are counted on one hand;
when your smiles, your tears
all add up the same.
I'll be that one place,
when your joys are mired in sorrows;
when you succumb to your tomorrows,
when you justify your crimes to place the blame.
I'll be that one place
when you gather up your senses,
when it's time to mend your fences;
when you realize that love is not a game.
I'll be that one place
when the world is full of danger,
when every friend becoems a stranger;
when those you've trusted
no longer know your name.
I'll be that one place
when you can no longer stand it,
when the fates, at last, command it;
when you can't see beyond the candles flame-
I'll be the soft place where you land.

I WON'T DRINK THE KOOL-AID

My thoughts are not in bondage.
My mind is my own.
My life cannot be gauged by rules
that I do not condone.
I learned as a little child
I must think for myself.
I cannot allow my psyche
to be abandoned on some shelf.
My soul is sequestered,
My heart is much too large;
my dreams cannot be placed on hold
with someone else in charge.
I am my own person.
I am master of my fate.
I must survive on my own terms
before it is too late.

MY GOD

My God,
is a gentle God,
a father to all men;
who, once has forgiven
will forgive again.
My God,
is a loving God,
who does not implore
a child of color
or one whose station we ignore.
My God,
is an understanding God,
who has reconciled
each one as worthy,
every child.
My God,
is a kind God.
My God, he commands
all men and women desire love-
my God understands.

THE LAIR

We are in a den of wolves.
The lambs are in disguise.
Too long, we have been wholly judged
by unsympathetic eyes.
We cannot flee before the flock
for we are mired in the field;
too involved to ever be
forced, by fear, to yield.

ILL WIND

My senses spin in chaos.
Anxious hands grapple the mattress
for fear of falling to the ceiling
as my world careens out of control.
Unfamiliar sounds,
a typhoon force,
negating my quiet mind.
A stillness that was my soul implodes-
a cataclysm of emotion.

IT'S NEARLY SPRING

(a sonnett)

It's nearly spring,
bid time return
to hedgerows lush with greenery,
to gardens where all maidens yearn
for long walks among daffodils-
easy moments of young love
while beads of fresh dew burn.
It's nearly spring,
all lovers speak
of secret moments meantfor two;
of secluded groves
romantics seek
to steal a kiss, to borrow time
where lowered eyes from shadows peek.
It's nearly spring,
how time has flown
from snowy breast to brilliant sun,
from coverlets on feather beds
when sweetest dreams are sewn,
where illusions meet reality
and sleeps memories are known.
It's nearly spring,
bid time presage
to tender blades pressed under foot,
too fragile blooms between each page
securing each breathless memory
enfolded in sighs, a notion
that when lovers eyes again engage
It's nearly spring.

I SANCTIFY

I sanctify
each eager kiss,
each trembling sigh of fresh romances.
I sanctify
each shrouded gaze,
each frighter reply
to fertive glances.
I sanctify
each love, so new,
each angels cry
of second chances.
I sanctify.

THE MOVIE, HAVING ENDED

The movie, having ended,
of love lost, love found . . .
I sensed a shadow follow me.
I turn, so slight, around.
The movie, having ended,
on one night in September,
reminding me of what had been mine-
love worthy to remember.
The movie, having ended,
moved my soul to song,
wrapping symphonies about me
urged me, play along.
The movie, having ended,
recalling you and me
weaving stardust and simple flesh
within what used to be.

AN OLD ROMANCE

An old romance
lingers on the screen,
reminding me of yesterday,
of what my memories mean.
An old romance
flickers in lights so dim,
noticing a shadow come so close
to feeling it is him.
An old romance
gutters to a lower flame,
barely casting images
before an ending came.
An old romance
gathers thin as dust,
collects in corners of regret
where every old love must.
An old romance
recalls the dreamers, yet,
each name, each face, every kiss
we must, finally, forget.

??????????????????????

We're cerated in Gods image-
be it your God or mine;
whether just, forgiving or vengeful,
are we spawned from the devine?
We're created in Gods image-
be it flesh and blood and bone;
whether spirit or immortal soul,
is this legacy our own?
We're created in Gods image-
be it angry, ferful, kind;
whether benevolent or vindictive,
is there no meeting of the minds?
We're created in Gods image-
be it far or narrow sighted;
whether temporate or jealous hearted,
are we inconstant,
thereby blighted?
We are created in Gods image-
be it Hell fire or elevated bliss;
whether gentle, proud or fickle,
are we predestined to this?
We're created in Gods image-
be it on you to decide;
whether your personal beliefs or mine,
are there any who abide?

SHE DANCES AS FAST AS SHE CAN

Ordained a thing of beauty,
resigned an also ran.
Perfection was her duty.
She dances as fast as she can.

Destined to such perfection.
First place was always the plan.
Facing the whole worlds rejection,
she dances as fast as she can.

Perceived as the one and the only,
illusion was her greatest fan,
She wanders the night oh, so lonely.
She dances as fast as she can.

Adored by those who don't know her.
Enamored of those in her clan.
She stoops, embracing those below her.
She dances as fast as she can.

Left to languish in sadness
while wasting away gaunt and wan.
Spinning and twirling toward madness,
she dances as fast as she can.

ON STAGE

Exit, stage left, the performance has ended.
Applause dies slowly amid the crowd.
Act one, scene one now commended.
Accolades offered out loud.

Each line committed to memory so
nuance achieved with aplomb.
Direction is given by mentors who know
what it feels like to finally go numb.

Every curtain call closes a new scene.
Admiration flows through every pore.
Alms adorn the new drama queen
who signs autographs at the door.

A star shines for the princess dramatic.
Crown her now amid these bright lights.
Curtains close and it's anticlimactic
in the shadow of opening nights.

PIRROUETTE

Pirrouette, plee' on a darkening stage,
bloodied feet, muscles tight as you move.
Too mature for a diva, a woman your age
like so many, you have more to prove.

Pirrouette, granjete' as the cutain comes down;
en point, what's the point of it all?
Just a chance as you dance
every person from town
will gather to witness your fall.

Pirrouette, arabesque, move against the spotlight.
Tulle and voile, you are dressed true to form.
Such a beauty on sight
you procure from the night
the power of heavenly storm.

Pirrouette, pretty feet, lovely hands;
you stand motionless upon the boards.
Leaping high, keep an eye
on uncertain demands
as you listen for opening chords.

Pirrouette as each note floats up from below.
Breathing deeply, you're ready to shine.
Left tonight, toe-to-toe
it is truely your show.
Prove your prowess to dance the devine.

Pirrouette, pirrouette move the audience yet
your ego is terribly bruised.
Twirl on toe, what's your point? Never fret.
There's no way to avoid feeling used.

Pirrouette, dance and spin
as you try to fit in.
Move your feet to a comfortable place.
To forgive any sin
forget where you'd begin
as you rest finally in fear and disgrace.

WINDOW PAIN

Standing on the outside looking in,
musing, there, about the state he is in.
Watching as his children laugh and play.
He wonders how it is she's spent her day.

Although it's a short time they've been apart.
He counts the pieces of his broken heart.
He misses her in sullen depths of night.
Wondering what to do to make it right.

"I'm sorry" isn't all he has to say;
wants her to know he loves her more each day.
He's on the out side, now,
he's looking in.
He wants his life back yet
where can he begin?
He stands there on the sidewalk of his life,
stares through the glass at his kids, his wife,
wondering if they'll be one again . . .
that must be why they call it window pain.

NO MOTHER SHOULD LOSE A CHILD

No mother should ever lose a child
to illness, accident, violence reviled.
She should surpass each in old age
when elements of time engage.

No mother should ever lose a child
ours to love unreconciled
to watch them on a path that's true
yet fate leaves little two can do.

No mother should ever lose a child
weaken ties of love anger-riled;
not let harsh words come between
the kinder words we really mean.

No mother should ever lose a child
owing love once reconciled.
But if they leave before you
remember everything they say and do.

TODAY MY DAUGHTER
RESTS WITHIN

Today my daughter rests within
my prayers protective shield.
I challenge any illness
to make her spirit yield.

Today my daughter rests within
good thoughts I send her way.
I plead for all that's positive
to keep all evil away.

Today my daughter rests within
the strength of caring hands.
I bid my love wrap 'round her
in binding golden strands.

Today my daughter rests within
the thoughts of those who care.
I join the positive, begin
to force away dispair.

Today my daughter rests within
the peace that courses through.
I bind her wounds, salve her pains.
it is the least I can do.

LONE GULL

A flock of gulls flies over the creek.
Naked trees stand, mute guardians
of the rusty benches under their
trembling arms.

The day is grim, dismal.

Somewhere below, gulls rest.
All but one, who flaps his weary wings,
gliding in endless spirals to the ground.
Changing direction, he moves upward again.

One lone gull sails undaunted.
The others rest unobserved.
Is he a loner or a leader?

DAY PASS FROM THE ASYLUM

A taste of freedom, of normal life;
a temporary respite from constraint.

Eight hours to breathe apart
from doctors, social workers.

Lunch, eaten out with family
who try to act as if everything is fine.

Conversations dance, lithe, around
uncomfortable topics,
never touching on the obvious.
Every comment soft, unfailingly cheery,
having a false ring to them.

You check the clock, eager to return.

HER LAST LOVER

She reached for him.
He glared at her.
Saying nothing, he was on his feet
and half-way down the beach
before she turned around.

Torn between relief and agony,
she watched his leaving.
She followed, waist deep in the soothing waters.
Each ripple seemed to caress, comfort.
Tender breezes kissed her face,
water lapped the tears from her eyes.

Surrendering to the sweet suduction of the night
to rest in the arms of her last lover.

ODE TO A STEEL WORKER

Six-foot-six
my husband stands
on the dock, unloading coal
fulfilling company demands
to save their corporate soul.

U.S.X./U.S.Steel
corporate heads extoll
unemployment's down this year
(so says the latest poll)
Six-foot-six
my husbans stands
on the dock, unloading coal
breathing gray, dull glittering dust
just shy of his fifteen year goal.
No one compensates black lung
once the union's lost control.

Great Lakes transport's on the rise!
Lake Erie's on a roll!
Six-foot-six
my husband stands
on the dock, unloading coal.

THIRD SHIFT

Eleven P.M. rears its nodding head
forcing open sleep-laden eyes.
Off to work one
goes alone off to bed–
one more night breathes a wistful goodbye.

HE'S DIVORCED, BUT . . .

There were nights in the old apartment
when we would be in bed,
you, asleep,
moonlight cascading through the window.
I would see your wedding ring
shining in thr darkness
and ache that it did not shine for me.

REVEREND

Spreading the word, of whom?
God? Jesus? Buddah?
What avatar metes out your support?
Shake your tamborine!
Pace and spew narrow doctrine
to ready ears, eager ears.
Say what moves them from pew to altar,
prostrate in abject humility, loosening
needless tears.
They worship the teacher in black dress
who capitulates no one.

MY DAUGHTER

She is an orchid.
A delicate soul, a tender spirit
Cloaked in a steely bravado,
talking tough but so easily wounded . . .
Each day she grows, changes,
emracing motherhood.
A grown up now.
I am so proud.

MITTENS

He looks into the eyes of a new cat,
watches movements, reads habits,
waiting patiently for her return,
gone these many years.
He must miss her terribly, he searches,
he puzzles so over every personality,
each quirky aspect.
His white calico with extra toes
who loved him best,
who was only his, his alone.
His Mittens.

WINDOW DRESSINGS

So often we judge others on how they look-
the right shirt, pants, tie;our hair just so . . .
Our attire somehow designates personality,
other attributes, good and bad.
Perhaps we should strive to be good
rather than looking good.

POOR WIDOW

Her shoulders curve under her burden,
tremendously her own.
Given succor by the caring,
her condition envelopes her.
A widow, now, she tarries over her plight,
stirring the pot on the front burner to a rolling boil.
Blend with care, women; you are not alone in your quandry.
What was it again?
Homelessness or sickness;
single motherhood, small child slung upon your hip? No.
Home intact, child, grown and gone . . .
secure and safe; stultified and bored.
A measured ploy, attention, undue care
commonly faced by stoic women
wholost husbands young, by accident
or absolution.
Half-couple, not half women.
Accept, graciously, when offered . . .
decline, out of hand, the unneccessary fawning:
stride, purposefully into the real world.
Disinterested, you insult the giving nature of truth.

CARRIED AWAY

Perfect spring rains linger
on days of careless joy.
Falling, child-like,
drops toy with forgetful blossoms.
Winds, a tell-tale reminder,
carry a single voice piercing
through the wisps of a song,
swept away by prattle of a
bright, smothering world.

CHLOE' KNOWS

When Chloe' smiles the world's alight
with wonders still to see through a
child's unerring eye.
Chloe's eyes take the magic in.
She sees what we will not
through our jaded sight.
Chloe' knows a special place
within her tiny grasp that evades
our reaching.
Chloe' holds the answers to happiness in her world.
She is willing to share her knowledge.
Chloe' sees what some are blinded by-
a brilliant, shining moment held within a smile.

WONDERING

Stretching out, midnight air wafting over supine forms,
I drift into dreams of girlhood friends, innocent pastimes.
Giddy tales of romance, musing over a first kiss, the
tender, clumsy touch of a hand . . .
Innocuous moments woven of innocent vulnerability.
So many years have slipped their hold on youth . . .
Finding love after long years, I wonder of my friend-
does her happiness equal teenage fantasy?
Is she hardened and wary of life?
She never speaks.
I wait in moments pulled together under moonlight
that lets me know the truth.

A MOTHERS LOVE

A mothers love can go so far
spanning space, time;
righting wrongs, drying tears,
making reason rhyme.
A mothers love, forgiving all,
a deference so slight
can bring misunderstanding,
make hands and muscles tight.
A mothers love can be confused
while trying to right wrongs,
when certain words were uttered
where some softer words belong.
A mothers love can break a heart
when meant to make amends
while efforts made, where efforts last
to quell the fire it rends.
A mothers love can be construed
as nagging vice to some.
Better bite down on your tongue
before the arguement is done.

WHAT'S SAID TODAY

Speak gently of me when I'm gone.
Let memories convey
the impact I had on your life
that led up to this day.
Remember all the good, the bad
with humor, with a laugh.
All your pain will drift away,
your anger, cut in half.
When you remenisce, I beg,
try to spesk your mind.
Yet, no matter what you think of me,
for anothers sake, be kind.
When moved to speak, but nothing good
comes to your mind to say,
take a breath, begin agsin.
Let it drift away.
If all you've known is pain and loss,
it was never my intent.
Now, is not the time, the place
to allow yourself to vent.
Someday you will understand
what you each have meant to me.
Until that moment, relax and know
that, finally, I'm free.
Share a story, tell a lie.
Add to no ones sorrow.
Remember, what you say today
will come back to you tomorrow.

LITTLE BOY

Where are you going, my little boy, little boy.
Blue eyes and blond curls,
where have you gone?
Your big and you're hateful,
you're so angry, too.
You think ill of everthing under the sun.
Where are you going, my little boy, little boy?
All dimples and laughter,
where have you gone?
You're depressed you're sad and unhappy
with life.
You're backed into a corner
with nowhere to run.
Where are you going, my little boy, little boy?
Your childhood is over, now, you're a man.
I don't know what happened
to make you hurt so . . .
I just know that you're running
as fast as you can.
Where are you going, my little boy, little boy?
Insecure and afraid, you're alone in your room.
Turn around where the light is.
There are people who love you.
There are people who can lead you out of the gloom.
Where are you going, my little boy, little boy?
the deck's not stacked against you.
The game isn't lost.
Turn your eyes to the light.
Let the light into your heart.
Let love be honest, whatever the cost.
Where are you going, my little boy, little boy?
Life's hard, but, there's something else
you'd better know . . .

Every secret you keep, every dream while asleep
will be left on your doorstep
wherever you go.
Where are you going, my little boy, little boy?
You're running, you're moving, you cannot keep pace.
Your deeds and your words
will take flight like the birds.
Heartache will find you in some other place.
Where are you going, my little boy, little boy?
Stand still, take a breath, take a good look inside.
Find out what you're doing, find out who you are.
The real you will find you wherever you hide.
Where are you going, my little boy, little boy?
Stand tall. Be a man. Be responsible now.
Take life as it comes. Don't complain of the turns.
You'll survive. You will make it somewhere, somehow.
Where are you going, my little boy, little boy?
My love will follow wherever you go.
I always have loved and will always love you.
I'm thinking of you more than you'll ever know.

A STEP BEYOND

Childhood ends.
The dreamer wakes, dreams left on his pillow.
The day breaks bright
soon after the night
leaves him more alone than you'll ever know.
A young man pulls the curtain back.
he stares as dew is burning.
A moment passed. It's time at last.
the morning leaves him yearning.
He's at the door. It's open now.
He knows why he has waited.
He moves at last. The moments past.
His appetite is sated.
There's progress made.
He's on the move.
No one will ignore him.
He's feeling great. He knows his fate.
His destinies implore him.
It's all laid out. The path is clear.
He's never going to stop.
The theory's moot. He knows the route.
He's headed to the top.
He cannot lose, He's prone to win.
The next move, only his.
He has worked hard. He holds the card.
He knows what winning is.

MANTRA FOR TOM

When good spirit fills the heart, the soul,
luck, the fates will follow.
All lifes positives will roll
to fill the void, the hollow.
A ring of gold will fill the land
with melodic aire.
Coin will fill each ready hand
fulfilling hopes of those who dare.
Coffers fill to overflowing.
Many dollars lilne the till
for the man who's in the knowing,
whose mantra says 'I will'.

LATE MAY MORNING

With damp, swet breath,
morning caresses with a breeze.
Dusky ribbons of light
edge the sky as day brinks.
Promise of rain, suspended
above the horizon,
wraps arms about the day
in languid embrace.
Birds call out from dewy coverings,
warbling incantations of new beginnings,
a greeting to the wakeful.
Sun evokes a promise-warmth, growth,
freshness from flower to fallow field.
New life reaches heavenward,
recovering from chill, damp night.
Greetings, whispers of air envelope brightness,
encouraging response of seeds, roots,
fertile soil orchestrated by the devine.

A DILIGENT GARDENER

He plants his seed in the garden
tenderly, row upon row,
embraced in the folds of fertile earth
gently encouraged to grow.
Cultivated, attended
nurtured, continual till.
Knowing that that preparation
enhances a God-given skill.
Kneeling, his offerings given
with knowledge, with so much
sacrificing time, giving talents
with a practiced touch.
Soiled hands may be washed clean,
a bended knee made straight
and yields of toiling efforts
will ultimately be great.
Seeing to fruition
a garden fuly grown
gives the satisfaction
of efforts rightly sewn.
Fragile stalks grown,
reaching high,
sturdy, green and tall . . .
grace and goodness given back
because one gave his all.

GRANDMAS GOWN

Yards of golden fabric
create a grandmas gown
as she adds her many stones
to make her sparkling crown.
Years have stitched together
a garment, shining bright.
Other grandmas know it
immediately on sight.
Each section of the pattern
enjoins a childs name,
a mantle so resplendent,
a maternal cloak of fame.
A new piece, added with great care
as each new babe is born,
never cumbersome, not heavy,
the most beautiful she'll ever know.
Gathering, for many years
to a glittering diadm;
assigned, at birth, a precious place
adds one more garnered gem.
Rich beyond all measure;
ignored by selfish fools,
a grandma holds a treasuer trove
of immortal jewels.
Each smile, each touch,
each little hand;
tiny arms that sweetly wrap
around granparents shoulders
as they curl up on their lap.

Binding past, the future, too,
girding to the present,
all golden, diamonds, joys
grandchildren represent.
Of all her great accomplishments,
she holds these things above-
nothing is as dearly held
as a childs love.
It is a garment that she wears
with esteem, with pride-
women embracing this part of life
with grandpa at her side.

LITTLE BOYS

Little boys, it seems, and dirt
have made a solemn pact
to darken faces, little hands
with every subtle act.
Each is drawn away from grass
to muck, to mire, to goo.
Moms endeavor to keep them clean
but there's nothing they can do.
They seem to attract each mess
grime is all we see
as they jump in puddles, sit in mud
with unadulterated glee.
Twirling in a cloud of dust,
pants torn, shirtsleeves stained;
inside each tiny gentleman,
a dirtball is ordained.
A mother must learn not to fret
lest she succumb to drink;
Knowing laundry additives
will save her from the brink
of suicidal tendencies,
of wash and wear travails,
the eagerness of little boys
to get filthy will not fail.
Just let the little ones go play.
Do not take them to task.
Requiring boys to stay clean
is just too much to ask.
So, let them play, have their fun.
Let the sun shine on.
Ther will be clean clothes a-plenty
when little boys are gone.

TODAY FOR MY MOTHER

TODAY,
I miss my mother.
No sunrise graced the morning as spring rain
pelted the patina of the highwauy outside my front door.
TODAY,
I'd like to pick up the phone with nothing particular to say
just for the closeness talking to her brings.
TODAY,
I would love to invite my mother to lunch. We would
gossip ans laugh and nearly forget our lunch, such fun
we would be having.
TODAY,
I would love to take my mother on a tour of the blossoming countryside,
    taking in the spring ambiance in my big, black
Cadillac, windows down, blowing back our hair.
TODAY,
I would like to wile away the twilight hours, sitting with my
mother, rocking slowly as we remember tender moments,
good and bad.
TODAY,
I would like to stroke my mothers hand as she wanders in dreams-but
    I can't.
My mother's been gone these many years,
taken young and suddenly.
But, yours is still with you, sometimes lonely anad out of palce;no longer
    home and never really graced with a solitary moment.
TODAY, embrace your mother, share a memory or two.
Pick up the phone, if for no other reason than to hear her voice.
When that voice is stilled, the quiet will be eternal.
Show her love is returned, unconditionally, in her waning days.
Forever is a long time to regret moments not spent on a busy day.

IN MY DREAMS, SHE WALKS

In my dreams, she walks,
(though Patti hasn't walked in years)
In my dreams, she walks—
no infirmities.
She laughs, dances . . .
Twenty-one was a lifetime ago.
In my dreams, she walks.
We are young and whole and vibrant.
Middle age has not touched us,
our bodies supple, new.
In my dreams, she walks.

LITTLE MEAN THINGS

Marge was never overtly cruel.
She did little mean things.
Fashioning a pink dress
leaving the pins in as a reminder.
Doling out love
one penny at a time-
alms for the poor box-
Altering a dress from size seven to two,
making it a one
squeezing out every breath.
Just little, mean things.
Paying for college with her approval,
shocked by apathy.
Her way or no way,
the constant inconstant.
The bar raised ever higher,
never content with best efforts.
Keeping wounds open with needling remarks, hurtful deeds.
Just little, mean things.

MINIMUM WAGE

Skies weep on,
streaking weary faces.
Cooling tears quench
fiery heads of summer.
All slows.
Time lags.
Edges of night, now liquid,
smear days median.
No music fills bleak voids
of inadequate warmth.
Pockets of color,
empty into a sorry purse,
sparing change of Spring.

TONY'S PRAYER

The coin of promise held in trust,
increases ten fold.
Held open, edges of a true heart
fill with honest gold.
Closed loosely,
gathers small offerings of greater gifts.
Kept close,
garners greatly
benefits of the blessed.

AS SISTERS

Each sister is giving, each sister is true.
Be gracious, be gentle in all that you do.
Extend a ready, eager hand to help in any task.
Be tender and be loving in questions that you ask.
Be sincere in service.
Be helpful and be kind.
Share a special little prayer
to ease a troubled mind.
We join in our humility,
hand-in-hand along the way
with a smile, a kindly word
to brighten someones day.

GIFT OF SPIRIT

When we are on our knees, dear Lord,
closed eyes, clasped hands, we pray.
Enlighten us with worthy thoughts
as we begin our day.
We seek a sacred wisdom
we have learned along the way,
repeated in humility
in all the words we say.
The scriptures are our G.P.S.,
our compass through the fray;
our bouy, our safe harbor
when we might drift away.
Our sincere tithes, our offerings
when complacency might sway,
we give our due to Father, God,
He asks and we obey.
Spiritual, temporal blessings
we don't need to assay.
They're added up celestially
where there is no delay.
For wordly goods, heavenly wares,
the other will hold fast, hold true-
gifts of spirit stay.

OCTOBER 31ST

Chill shoulders shrug scarlet leaves,
a cloak about the feet.
Gray eyes blink through cool tears, streaking colors.
Heady loam scents fields, pastures
mowed one last time.
Mums, pumpkins dance in festive breezes
lifting faces toward a dimming sun.
Cotton clouds shake tentative snows
to cooling green,
resting an instant to the eye.
Naked limbs embrace a changing sky.

A CASH FLOW PROBLEM

Two cents to rub together,
a pocket with a hole;
too many debits and no credits
are bound to take its toll.
When cash flow is a hemorage,
you cannot staunch the flow
of every dollar drained away
with nothing left to show.
To be nickled, to be dimed to death,
good money after bad.
Two nickles rubbed together
was all the sense we had.
We feed the pig.
We go for broke.
We save and save and save.
Our balance forward is a joke
with the interest that they gave.
The column's long,
the ink is red-
if only it were black . . .
Then, there'd be plenty to withdraw,
alas, it's funds we lack.

TURN AWAY

Turn away from the night,
the tight embrace of death;
long arms tightening
to squeeze out every breath.
Unveil the stars,
unfold the sky.
The path to chart is clear.
The distance between two points depends
upon what you hold dear.
Daybreak rolls in twilights wake,
washing past gritty sands.
Time moves on, as we all do,
unclasping eager hands.
Close the door on darkness.
Let the light seep through.
Gossimer folds of daylight
drape lightly about you.

1000 EASY STREET

In my back yard is a money tree.
(my children all think so)
They must believe their bullshit
is what makes its grow and grow.
"Can I borrow twenty, Mom?
"I'll pay you backnext week."
They'd better pray my oil well
never springs a leak.
They seem to think my purse contains
pure gold by the ounce
and, that I have a great big check
that will never bounce.
What if we're evictedfrom our house on Easy Street?
Will they give a fortune
to each con man that they meet?
The diamond mine has petered out.
The piggy bank is smashed.
Still, they have their hand out
just as our check is cashed.
We'd like to put a bit aside
for some rainy day
in case opportunity
is one sailed ship away.
If you see me on some corner,
tin cup in my fist,
I'm only trying to finance
my grown up kids wish list.
If beggers can't be choosers,
the evidence will show
the winners and the losers
are everyone we know.
I'll shove my hands in pockets, deep,
come out without a cent.
There'll be no inheritance-
it's already spent!

FIRST FALLING

First snow clings to tentative branches,
a sugar coating,
finely sifted over fallen leaves, parked cars.
Drivers forget old skills,
swerve and slip over slick patina.
Wipers, in syncopated time
to road splash, small rivlets from the roof,
squeak in unison.
Heaters blast, tires thrum through salt, ash and cinders.
Gloved hands gripthe wheel.
Tense necks react.
All roads lead to parking
where plows heave great dunes of gritty borders.

IGNORED BEQUEST

My childhood home of happy troubles
is in the family.
Passed to the eldest son of the son-not to me.
Lush greens, pastel peach blossoms ignored, lost.
No tender beries explode across the field,
clinging to prickly switches, nor hang
heavily from a mulberry bough.
Fragrant loams hide under thickets
and young wood where vegetables
used to flourish.
No grazing ponies or caged rabbits
shear the rambling lawns
Where rose of sharon, lilac,
would waft, stubby striplings quiver, naked.
So many nights from my east-facing room
I'd dream of seamless summers full of flowers and berries;of great green
    expanse; of sour cherries, tart quince.
So much magic packed into yearning acres.
The old, brown house would creak and groan
with each seasons change, window staring
across the valley to town.
Subtle sunsets draped the bluff as I wandered
with Gobi into summer nights.
I only visit Welton Road in the steep climes
of night when gracious dreams, giddy illusions
wish me back to steady comforts of childhood.
Girls marry, move away, good for little else
while ungrateful sons, unworthy,
command the tool shed and ramble through the big,
cold house alone.
No parties, no picnics;no card games, no fights
or celebrations.
The big house, reinvented, marks time, stuck
in an uncomfortable place.
Giving nothing back of its past, foreseeing no future.
The top of the hill, the end of the road,
dark in solitude . . . illuminated in memory.

STASIS

Empty arms, a scant embrace, cools in memory.
A touch, a look, a tender word prevails upon my heart.
Dreams revisit passions in stasis,
a dimly lit limbo where images fade untouched.
Swallowed kisses choke back seamless lips.
Linear faces, drawn tight across a smile,
turning down each request.
Spirits carry fragile egos, tether hearts across the years.
Moments found alone, together, weave a cozy shroud
keeping ids intact.

TO BETTY ANN MC

Early in my high school days,
back in 1971,
I thought girls like Betty Ann
were having all the fun.
Until
we found ourselves disolved in tears,
our under eyes a mess.
Betty Ann,
dabbing tissues underneath her eyes
before the mirror,
poised in her mini dress
proclaimed
"mascara burns when you cry."

RESTLESS NIGHTS

A sleepless night, a dream unknown.
No rest for the weary.
The clocks tick on, skies open to
daybreak with tired eyes.
Deep night burns away to ash
as old bones rise.
Days brink, ready or not.
Slow motion catches the eye
of the well-rested.
Shuffling steps puncuate a yawn.

MY SON, THE DAD

He fills the role made just for him.
His shoulders square, hands steady;
eyes wide with wonder with attention to every detail.
He's a father—no—he's a dad.
Being a dad requires more than agreeable biology.
A dad must listen for subtle cries, at the ready for scraped knees,
bumped heads and gas.
Fits of temper never sway, soon forgotten.
Dads never yell(he may raise his voice)
Slights irritate but quickly pass.
Appreciation for refridgerator art
surpasses all other forms.
Lullabyes will be learned by heart and missed
when replaced by whatever is popular at the time.
A dad loves unconditionally, knowing his childs
beauty and wit are the only truths worth knowing.
Dads stay up late and get up early and sometimes
makes pancakes.

SMALL WONDERS

Wonders never cease.
How can one child's beauty
outshine anothers when they, too,
are the epitome?
How can the bluest eyes
eclipse two eyes bluer still?
Tufted heads, so downy;
fragrant skin so fresh, so new
to old nostrils yet remembered from
another time . . .
How can anything so small
be considered big or long?
Barely secured in the crook of an elbow
seems tiny indeed.
Are we so fickle? Or, do we fail to remember
each new child is a fresh blossom,
sprouted anew for old senses?
A new life, a fresh start, a clean page
on which to inscribe the future.

CHRISTMAS COOKIES

I've always preferred to work alone,
entrenched on baking day.
Until Gabe said "Grandma, can I help?"
Well, what could I say?
My kitchen is awash with flour,
egg shells crunch below.
Brightly colored cookies line
mis-shapen in a row.
I think he ate two chocolate chips
for each one put in the mix,
There was nothing done so wrong
that grandma couldn't fix.
I'll have a precious memory
for each cookie that he cuts.
The dog has had his fill today
of cookie dough and nuts.
Gabes hands, his face, his shirt's a mess-
he's cookie, head to toe.
This memory means more to me
than he will ever know.

FROM ORANGE COUNTY

The crime of innocense, punished by inhumanity,
a punishment not vsited on animals.
Children deliver us from our frailties
by virtue of their spirit.
Their guiless smiles, their eager eyes,
know all our weaknesses.
Sadly, the wrong people are blessed-
the undeserving, unappreciative
who care more for shallow pursuits
than for the honest love of a child.
Looking into our faces with abject trust,
they are ignorant of the peril
of trusting too much.

RESPITE

Gray days beckon,
prelude to the new year.
Winter rains pelt,
temporate winds buffet scant trees.
Clumps of grimy snow, now slight,
greets us
as we move about, coats open
to the pretense of better weather.
Soon, flurries will circle our bare heads again
while we curse what's normal.

UNDER THE RADAR

Being always aware, glancing back, over my shoulder,
vigilant of my surroundings.
I check my motions, my motive,
just to be safe.
I am weary of the sport.
Only one step away from ruin,
one breath from disaster,
keeping a harried pace.
I check my rear view mirror
I start at passing cars.
I keep my profile low,
under the radar.

FAREWELL TO ADAM

So, you've moved on, old friend.
I will miss our comfortable routine,
our easy conversations.
I could always settle within your care,
pulling your kindness about me,
a cozy quilt of vibrant color.
Your smile has been pressed between
the rustling pages of my days.
You will resurrect in my thoughts,
while your replacement is weighed
on an unjust scale.
You will remain my sparkling beacon,
illuminating a path to sanity in this crazy life.
I wish you well.

JANUARY 09

Tera firma crackles under my tires
as I back from my drive.
6a.m. horizons brink crisp, clean.
A taunting half-moon gapes the
sparing stars, braving the cold.
The bank sign reads 14-.
Frigid breath wraps everything.
Snow plows scrape,
sparking dark betweenblade and
asphault-
a celebration of deepest winter.

A WASTED DREAM

You had a dream,
an ability you were born with . . .
A little training and you could have excelled.
But, for some reason,
whether time or finance or circumstance,
these things were put on hold.

Your visions roll about your head.
You imagine what could be
just before it becomes what might have been.
You never take the next step.

God can only do so much.

He had a plan for you.
He gave you all the tools to accomplish each
task at hand.
If you choose to sit and imagine
where you could have gone,
what you could have been
without ever using the talents you were
born with,
then you have not only cheated yourself,
but, the universal power that makes great things possible
with a little effort on your part.

ONE HOT MAMA

Grandma was one hot mama-
bottle of Frank's Hot Sauce,
jar of pepperocinis-
Minnie liked it hot.
Grandma put hot sauce on everything.
Her chili made your ass breathe fire
She left me all her recipes,
her knack for fiery Irish foods.
I don't know where she got it.
Legend has it,
Minnie had an Italian aunt.
Grandma could cook,
that is all I know.
I loved Grandma.
Through me, her baked beans are legend.
She lives through me.
I hope I pass on a little of her incendiary methods
to my son.
He cooks, he eats, he enjoys.
Minnie would have called him "Bucko"
Grandma was one hot mama.

GHOST OF A CHANCE

Children notice even when we think they don't.
Each nuance, every variable-
aware of subtlties . . .
We will be held accountable
for all future transgressions.
Our failures will comeback to haunt us
when we least expect it.

VALORS DREAMS

She expresses sadness
for things so deeply loved.
No joy springs
from lovely things
held close to her heart.

Anguish bleeds from her heart
as she writes of her desires.
Feeling sad
when experience had
should lift her soul to song.

She aches with terrible loss
for what she's never had
because she knows it's impossible.

She doesn't grasp the singular joy
of the day to day,
a happy strand
into her hand
escapes her tenuous grasp.

A stallion in a sunny field,
two little foals at play-
no other charms
will fill her arms
She's desolate at the loss.

She holds no hope of attaining
the beauty her life lacks,
It would take a toll
were she to extoll
a dream that won't come true.

FAMILY IS MORE

Family is more than viscous fluid
coursing throughg arteries,
more than all memory or genetic markers.

Family, never trussed by filial ties
nor tethered by proximity,
brought closer than flesh and marrow.

Like spirits bind us one to another,
sister to brother,
kin of circumstance.

Banding together to be enriched
by experiences, by commonality.

Joining a clan of believers
striving for goals,
traveling like paths,
born by support, faith, love.
Relative trekkers along a trail of trust,
nurturing, growing, strengthening self-
greet the weary who arrive with fanfare,
friendship,
embracing all who come to partake at their table.

THE GOOD MAN

He goes to work each morning.
He come straight home each night.
He scans the vast horizon
while never losing sight
of his lifes true purpose,
of all that living means
even when the times are tough,
when all he has are dreams.
If he fears, he does not show it.
Anxiety is quelled
by all the love he has in life,
by all the love that's held
in his husband-fathers heart
for his children and his wife.
They are the reason for each breath,
the impetous of life.
Each soft caress has meaning
as does each loving smile.
He keeps them tethered to his heart,
safe keeping for awhile.
His coffers, overflowing.
His assets are so vast.
He has true love in his life;
a treasure that will last.
His value, plain and simple,
is that of one good man
who, when asked to move a mountain,
will do the best he can.
He rises before sunrise
where lonely shadows lurk.
Smiling, as the day begins,
he's heading off to work.
He goes to work each morning.
He comes straight home each night
to see the beaming faces who
make everything alright.

COMMITTMENT

Animals are innocent.
We catch them up in our lifestyles,
training them to fit our needs.
They comply, all functions according to our schedules.
We put them in a dependent position and become annoyed
at the inconvenience of their existence.
When they are no longer cute or cuddly,
we ignore their needs,
turning from the love they so willingly give.
The worst of us cast them aside
to shelters or faraway farms or secluded niches where their
abandonment
goes unnoticed.
All of these options are wrong.
When we adopt our animals,
we make a committment to care, to nurture, to protect.
We accept the unconditional love
and must balance our time to make sure their lives are safe,
secure.
They would never reject us or lose interest
because we age or become infirm.
They will be there for us.
We must be there for them.

GOBI'S TIME WITH THE ANTHONYS

(twenty years ago remembered)

He stands in the corner of the paddoack,
back turned against the storm.
He wishes he was in the barn,
dry and safe and warm.

It's been several days since she abandoned the horse
there irregardless of the weather
as if she didn't care.
A bale of hay and a bucket of water
were left for him that night.
She never cast a backward glance
as she drove out of sight.

She didn't really own the horse,
he was only leassed.
'She grew weary of demands
and wished to be released.

He'd served her for the summer.
His usefullness had passed.
She'd return him to his owners
now the seasons past.

A horse can only do so much
if a rider can't excell
If they don't know what they're doing
a smarter horse can tell.

He'll wait for the storm to end.
He aches, he stands alone
remembering how he was loved
when he was at home.

DIXIE

She was a little girls best friend,
bestowing time, attention and treasured castoffs-
a smudge of lipstick, an old purse, a dab of perfume . . .
moments spent.

Her accepting smile meant more than words
from any other grownup.
There was an unconditional trust,
a special care that shimmered into the deep and lonely nights
of misunderstanding that enveloped the world
lingering long after childhood ended.

BALDYS (A LITTLE BIT OF HEAVEN)

We'd spend the day at Baldys farm,
a heady, fun-filled day.
Ma and Eve canned pickles;
Baldy and 'Hoppy' Dad and Clyde baled hay.

Gary and I rode horseback throughout the fields.
Judy gathered clovers before we were called in for meals.

Rusty was a rotund horse that I would always ride.
My pudgy legs would stick straight out
from his broad back, side-to-side.
My appetite was whetted then.
A passion on its course.
I knew that I could not give up
until I had my own horse.

I'd brush Rusty's spotted belly.
I'd muck his dirty stalls.
I'd spend my summer days with him
in smelly overalls.

Eve and Baldys big, old farm
of childhoods paradise-
If told that I could never leave,
I would not have to think twice.

Lucky, Rusty, Cavalier
winnied as we passed.
All indelible memories
that fill my childs past.

Baldy, Eve, the farm, all gone,
mouldering to dust.
The pasture fence has fallen down,
broken posts and rust.

But deep within my heart of hearts
the barn swallow sings his song,
In the great barn of my memory
they're mine and they live on.

MA JONES

Three quarters of the way down Welton road,
sat a gray shingled house
inside a lovely yard.
Across the front was a sun porch
where Ma Jones raised her birds.

Walking passed heralded fanfares of chirps
and Ma Jones' tender words.

Parakeets, canaries, cockatiels
sang and chattered on.
Ma Jones cared for them
from morning until dawn.

There was nothing of domestic birds
that she didn't know,
From protected hutches,
gorgeous birds would show.

When my memories drift to Mae Jones,
I smell flowers in the back.
I see her chiuaua in the yard.
I touch the lovely handkerchief
she sent in every card.

Ma Jones was a special gem of our neighborhood-
wife, mother, friend-
forever doing good.

Ma Jones is gone.
Her house remains
but, now there is no song.
Just dirty windows and an empty porch
where chirping birds belong.

TRICK OR TREAT

If you go out on the streets today,
you surely won't be alone.
You'd better stay off the streets today.
You'd just better stay at home.

With all of the crowds and all of the fuss,
it's beggers night, it's all of the buzz.
Tonight's the night the kids all go trick-or-treating
The ghosts and the ghouls in the town turn out-
more devils and demons than you can count.
Witches surely dandle about.
Today's the day the kids all go trick-or-treating

Monsters, scary faces abound;
creatures creep to chill and astound
with plenty of candy to pass all around.
Today's the day the kids all go trick-or-treating.

It's Halloween, it's the thirty-first
when every vampire is quenching his thirst,
to scare us all they'll be doing their worst.
Today's the day the kids all go trick-or-treating.

For every princess and every hag
who has a candy filled plastic bag
that's so heavy that they all seem to drag.
Today's teh day the kids all go trick-or-treating.

OF PROMISES AND DUST

You broke another promise. dear,
in truth, I have lost track
of all your broken vows, thus far,
of pledges taken back.
You offer alms in all good will
and you mean to follow through
each of your agendas
every contract made by you.
You find yourself conflicted
and your lust, your greed, devours
any demand of your time,
of minutes and of hours.
I forgive you, daughter.
I'll not take you to task.
I know you are incapable
of giving what I ask.
I know you mean well in your heart;
your pledge, your recompense . . .
somehow you cannot follow through
or make any sense
for every broken promise,
for each dream you render gone.
I'll love you, no matter what
when our time on earth is done.

OUR INNER TRUTH

No matter how good we think we are,
No matter the guise shown to others,
our inner truth, our blackened heart
grabs hold of us and smothers
every good intent, each unselfish thought.
For every sacrificial act,
our inner truth eclipses these,
revealing frailties fact.
We are not so pure aas we suppose.
We are not unsullied in our souls.
Our inner truth reveals and we
are forbidden to be whole.
Do we suppose there is a Hell,
a place of damned unrest?
Our inner thoughts declare thus far
by our guilty hearts bequest.
We struggle so to keep afloat.
We are but earthly sons and daughters,
Our inner truths bouy, weight us down
in our transgressions waters.
No matter how we say our prayers,
no matter how many guilty tithes we pay,
our inner truth pronounces
each unkind word we say.
We are not allowed to hide the truth.
We are revealed behind our masks . . .
our inner truths for all to see
behind favors that we ask.
No matter number of good deeds,
no matter, how the columns add,
our inner truth reveals to us
each sacrifice we've had.
The secret, prideful heart can find . . .
we are the sum, the total
of deeds, of trials won . . .
our inner truth before us,
we meet God when life is done.

OH, BABY GIRL

Oh, baby girl, I see your face.
I recall a childs embrace;
a love so pure cannot erase
the deeds that have been done.
O, baby gril, such innocense-
our losses cannot recompense
actions gone against good sense
when wrongs can't be undone.
Oh, baby girl, I truly love
angelic souls sent from above,
who yielded when push came to shove
when she was the only one.
Oh, baby girl, now you have grown,
with little children of your own.
You reap the seeds that you have sewn.
Resigned, what's done is done.
Oh, baby girl, the road is rough
when all you've given is not enough;
fires of sorrow rendered tough
your travels toward the sun.
Oh, baby girl, I won't ask why
you're satisfied to frown, to cry,
to ponder as your life goes by
when tomorrow's yet begun.

HOW DO WE DO IT?

How do we hide what we know is true?
How does honesty reveal who we are?
How do we bring to earth
our celestail worth
while gazing at a star?
How do we conceal what is a fact?
How do we condone a lie?
How do we admit our failings
while our truths assailings
as we're trying to just get by?
How do we admonish greed and pride?
How do we sacrifice our grief?
How do we accept what we have lost,
accept the heavy, crushing cost
of exposing our belief.
How do we reveal to our friends?
How do we tell our family?
How do we admit we are but flesh
while shames enmesh,
we succumb to frailty?
How do we subjugate ourselves to prayer?
How do we drop down to our knees?
How do we bless
those having less
while we hide from all God sees?
How do we ask forgiveness?
How do we receive Gods grace?
How do we guess
what saints redress
to meet God face-to-face?

How do we make our just amends?
How do we ask God to forgive?
How do we plead
for all we need
to succeed, to breathe, to live?
How do we give more of ourselves?
How do we sacrifice?
How do we look before we leap
to make only promises we can keep,
to act before thinking twice?
How do we give of ourselves only ?
How do we offer more?
How do we give
so more will live
while other souls ignore?
How do we garner goodness?
How do we do good deeds?
How do we know
what lacks don't show
of every human need?
How do we rejoice in wisdom?
How do we enjoy the thought?
How do we make amends;
consider all men friends
having lost each battle fought?

INCUBUS

I was visited by love,
an ardore past, long dead, resurrected on this night.

A hand, in darkness, covers me,
reminding of some bliss past
within my failing sight.
So many years have ebbed away.
Each hour drifts to days
of loss condemning right.
From time-to-time I remember
a kiss, a touch, embrace
treasured in hindsight.
Somewhere in my broken heart,
I'm mended for a time
as memories hold me tight.

MUSIC

The spaces between each note
fill me with anticipation for the next.
Each half, each whole, each quarter note
builds suspense,
carrying across chasms of longing-
the next bar, coda begs repeating . . .
A breeze of musicality,
lifting to heights
man cannot aspire but for
the rhapsodies, of harmonies
blending perfectly in mid-air.

SUDDEN FALL

Yesterday, the leaves hung green
from sturdy stems.
Today, they blaze a scarlett that
a supple tree condemns.
Soft, moist young grasses
stretch beneath our feet
awaiting autumn foliage
as cooler weeks repeat.
Setting suns these dwindling days,
soft horizons in decline,
slightly out of balance seems
adrift without design
Just a breath ago, such heat
of summer scorched the days
with sufficating gasps of air
encouraging delays.
Thus, activities begin apace
with goods fair weathers sell
to every eager troubador
their burning stories tell.

FATE RELENTS

All things change, age, grow old;
termination cedes.
We plod along from day to day.
attending to the needs
of our children, as they're growing,
of our family, as a whole,
believing all the good we do
will save our withering soul.
We glean our happy endings
from fields quite ripe with pain.
Cultivate when planted,
grown full of weeds again.
We puzzle as to know the scope
of everything we've done
to realize quite suddenly
we are not number one.
No thing on earth is static.
All things are in flux.
We question order in our life
to move into the crux.
Forward motion is a must,
each inch, each increment
bares us ever onward
until the fates relent.

EULOGY FOR MA

I once had a friend
who was hurt because his family
treated him as an outsider-
I understood too well.
But, I told him that family
is not decided by flesh and blood,
but, rather a family is defined by depth
and scope of feeling and caring and unconditional love.
Today, we gather, friends and family;relatives and relative
strangers.
And, today we gather here carrying a sack
of memories, good and bad.
This little sack may hold anger and fear; resentment and, if we
are lucky, some aspect of love.
Whatever our own sack contains,
I have this to say:
If you have never hurt another—physically, emotionally;
materially or spiritually-
if you have never raised your hand in anger,
never lashed out at an undeserving child or adult-
If you have never gained (no matter how slight)
unjustly-
If you have never spoken in anger words you would soon
regret-
if you have never acted out of greed or selfishness,
never bruised an ego or crushed a spirit;
broken a heart or caused a tear to fall-
I say 'God bless you'

We are in the company of saints or liars.
Today, we have the chance to cast aside those little
sacks and free ourselves to forgive wrongs, real
or imagined, and make peace with the past.
And, on remembering our own humanity, we must
remember the human frailties of others.
Look, as you leave, at your children and grandchildren and
know: As they grow, their capacity to give, and show
love and to ultimately receive love-
is directly related to the love they have been given
and the manner in which it has been shown-
So, as we say good-bye to Ma, Grandma, Evelyn . . .
remember . . . that quilt or dress she sewed
or that special cake or pie she baked.
She did the best she could with what she had.
A person can only return the love they receive in the circle of life.
Remember, she loved us all in her own way, the only way
she knew.
We cannot learn what we are never shown-
If some of you today cannot bring yourselves to release
your anger, resentments and old hurts;feeling somehow righteous
and comfortable and safe-by allmeans, hold them close and tight-
just remember, that whatever you put out into this world
will return to you someday.

MY DAUGHTER

My daughter is a beauty-
not of heart, but face.
Yet, a dark, a brooding soul
belies her outward grace.
My daughter had a sparkle,
by her demeanor spoke
of all her good intentions
when evil deeds invoke
a troubling, errant picture
of true beauty cast aside.
Some kernal of an angel
dressed in fire must reside
with a nature-nurture,
with an element of care,
days within the damaged husk
amid our prides despair
exits the remnants of a girl
whose future was once bright.
Now, eclipsed by some dark force
lays trapped within the night.
My daughter breezes by in life
between happiness and loss,
when her deeds catch up to her,
she hangs on her own cross.
My daughter has become a trial,
a test that love must take.
All pray to get a passing score
for enmities sake.
Some suffer greatly at her hand
as beauty hides what's real.
Covert truths creep warily
ingrained in all who feel
taken in by avarice,
by lovely, dark demand.

Please tell me. God, what dire event
wrested kindness from her hand?
Can she be so lost to us?
Can her outlook be so bleak
to damn us and she eternally
to a loss we cannot speak?
We must embrace the good, the bad;
the beauty and the beast,
resigned that she has taken all
while giving up the least.
She Remains a thing of beauty,
a diamond in the rough.
Life may offer everything
yet, she'll never have enough.

SLEEP?

Tonight, as many gone before,
slumber hides behind a door;
locked to me while I implore
the elements for sleep.
Tonight, I starve, I hunger more
for a spate of dreams, for I am poor
of treasure rested heads ignore
gluttonous for sleep.
Tonight, tonight, I do yearn for
the drifting from one nights decor
to find peace on some distant shore
known to those who sleep.
In bed with lovers I adore
developing such sweet rapport
to toss, to turn it is a chore
to pretend to sleep.
Though pills and potions by the score,
I embrace what late night has in store.
The aspect of my purse is dour-
I cannot fall asleep.

OH, PILGRIM

Oh, Pilgrim, do not follow me
for I am very lost, you see;
too lost to follow faiths decree-
belief at any cost.
Oh, pilgrim, faithful, good and just
by your doctrine, souls are trussed
to testify passages discussed-
belief at any cost.
Oh, pilgrim, as we travel near
to destinations not so clear,
you find the promised land so dear-
belief at any cost.
Oh, pilgrim, testify, hold fast
to revelations of the past.
Go down fighting to the last!
Belief at any cost.
Oh, pilgrim, do not follow me,
for I am not who I seem to be.
I yearn for faith to set me free-
belief at any cost.

PARTICIPATE IN LIFE!

Dear friend, what council can I give
to cause your soul to lift, to live,
to rise up from your dusty bed?
Participate in life!
What can be said to sway your mind
to say 'go look' to say 'go find'
the happy dreams that you desire?
Participate in life!
Can I persuade you 'take a chance'?
Lift your feet until you dance!
Participate in life!
My friend, you must stay awake
to keep the promises you make.
Life passes as you lie abed.
Participate in life!
Do not let life pass you by
as you sit alone and cry;
while you wallow in your grief.
Participate in life!
Take a breath, invoke some peace
to grant yourself deserved release.
take your destiny in hand.
Participate in life!
Take a walk, talk to a friend.
Bring your seclusion to an end.
You've taken toomuch time to grieve.
Participate in life!

OCT. 31ST

Halloween brings little feet
door-to-door for trick or treat.
Cold or rain cannot defeat
the quest for any sweet.
Halloween brings ghosts and ghouls
following the dark night rules
to gather bags of tasty jewels
with disguises for their tools.
Halloween brings every child
as witches, devils reconciled
with every demon once reviled
happy children now run wild.
Hallowen brings nymphs and sprites
traipse rustling leaves this deepest night
alas, as with the full moons plight
all revelers flee from sight.
Halloween endures
for what is rend
an evening spent with every friend
to gather gifts, to recommend
a smile for dimes we spend.
Halloween brings to our door
elves and imps who thus implore
to offer goods they're searching for
with joy hard to ignore.
Halloween for all who say
one must venture forth into the fray
to leap, tolaugh without delay
this last October day.

SHE

She bandies, infirm, yet, resolute.
All her handicaps refute
queries of the more astute-
doing good for what it shows.
She does no good for goodness sake
but for the reputations make
her own lack to numb, to slake
her fates endenture grows.
She won't commit, not 'no' not 'yes'
she tries but she cannot confess
her crimes against the powerless
whose damage no one knows.
She dandles from her perch while she
enjoys what can be gleaned for free.
She fails to be what she claims to be
offering crumbs to hungry crows.
She holds past deeds inside her heart
to pick, to choose yet, never start
culpable she sets apart
her highs devoured by lows.
She was wrong but won't admit
why she was deemed as one unfit
to be a mother, requisite
Somewhere a child grows.
She set apart so willingly
all maternal aspects she
betrayed a trust so wrongfully
reaping what she sews.

She cannot admit the wrong
that haunts her, vexes all along
stifling the hearts own song
She wrestles in deep throes.
She has children, yet there's none
to comfort her when life is done
unworthy of the prizes won
her darker sides don't show.
She may be lonely, may be blessed
without remorse her sins redressed.
She will never find true rest
that is how Karma goes.

WHEN ANGELS SING TO ME

When angels sing to me
I must ranscribe the score;
must listen as the music of the spheres
offers beauty none ignore.
When the angels sing to me,
of Heavenly Fathers words
transported by the beauty
of every thing I adore.
When angels sing to me,
my nights belong to God.
His stars, his moon bequeathes to me
the blessings dreamers laud.
When angels sing to me,
my heart recites by rote
each chorus, every melody
composed there note-by-note.
When angels sing to me
I will not delay
I join in their celestial song.
I celebrate the day.
When angels sing to me
I am safe from earthly harms
Heavenly Father gathers me
into protective arms.
When angels sing to me,
no lesser souls contrive
to chasten me to thus ignore
when scriptures come alive.
When angels sing to me
they regale a story
point to the path we all must take
to deserve celeastial glory.

When angels sing to me,
all the world holds still
that I may hear the music,
that I may know his will.
When angels sing to me
I forsake what's passed
embracing all the gifts of life-
gifts of heaven last.

GIVE/TAKE

We cannot take it with us.
Wealth stays when we die.
We are not what we have given
but the' how' the 'why'.
Do our gifts flow from guilty waters
as we flounder in remorse?
Given freely, no restrictions
we let Karma run its course.
As we clutch a bulging purse,
held tightly by its strings,
unwilling to loosen straining cords
for the rewards the giving brings.
Some are destined to give advice
while some are here to take.
Decide if you are willing
to give for the giving sake.
It' s not unkind to answer 'no'
to another souls request-
If you, yourself, contribute
when you believe yourself a guest.
Do you darken someones door
for company or meals?
How you repay a kindness
is what your act reveals.
Your true, your sure intentions
when you accept from those who lack
not for a breath considering
you should give something back.

THE TRAGIC HEART

She didn't cause the injury.
She hid behind her skirt.
She failed to move, she failed to act
thus, she leveled hurt.
She was deaf to all the cries
muffled by closed doors.
She could have rescued, surely,
as maternity implores.
She stood still to save herself,
her conscience reconciled.
It seemed to cause her little grief
to sacrfice her child.
She'd cleave unto her husband
though she knew all along
that what he'd done was heinous,
protecting him was wrong.
Powers that be relieved her
of a mothers grace.
No absolution of the heart
could permit her crimes erase.
In her soul she gave to him
what ill deeds should not bring
She lit the flames upon the pyre
She let the death knell ring.
She has lost forever,
her consequence is grief
bound by law to grant them
some semblance of relief.
She feathers her empty nest.
All her doves have flown
because she uses ignorance
of things she should have known.
She caused her pain, her sadness.
Her children, now, are gone.

They had to sacrifice their past
for their future to move on.
She admits to no one close
nor feels the need to start
to claim herself responsible
for every tragic heart.

ON SUNDAY, SOME ARE BLESSED

On Sunday, some are blessed
to embrace a day of rest
they sleep the day away.
On Sunday, some are blessed
to repair the week-long dwindling zest
to spend the day at play.
On Sunday, some are blessed
refraining from their toil lest
we cave to societies request
to just enjoy the day.
On Sunday, some are blessed
to search their soul for Heavens quest
that they not go astray.
On Sunday, some are blessed
to give to the Lord at his behest
in grace, in peace the day.
On Sunday, some are blessed
teach the young to pass the test.
We act upon the words we say.
On Sunday, some are blessed
to love the ones who left the nest
to finally find their way.
On Sunday, some are blessed
to forego the worlds bequest
saving Sabbath as His day.

ELIZABETH THE FIRST

Born of noble blood to grace
fiery tresses framed her face.
Hers was a kingdom to embrace-
Elizabeth the First.

Born of noble blood to fame
millenia would speak her name.
The English empire would never be the same.
Elizabeth the First.

Born beneath a noble star,
she would excell, she would go far.
Her skills led the English where they are-
Elizabeth the First.

Born of blessings she'd presage
the era known as the Golden Age.
The powers that she would engage-
Elizabeth the First.

Born of power, known as heir,
accomplishments none could compare;
the heritage gleaned from her care-
Elizabeth the First.

Born to be the greatest queen,
to guide the people in between
lack of plenty they had seen-
Elizabet the First.

Born to make her country proud,
her name the world proclaimed aloud;
loved, admired by the crowd-
Elizabeth the First.

Born to prove inherent worth,
to rule the greatest power on earth;
succeeded men who saw but dirth–
Elizabeth the First.

Born to grow without mother,
to subjegate sister after brother;
She'd rule incomparably as no other–
Elizabeth the First.

BROKEN DOLL

Envied by many for her face,
epitomized quiet style, grace;
inner beauty could not replace
what terror stole from her.

She was all beauty could embrace
on every path her steps would trace.
Born of muslin, deserving lace
before terror stole from her.

Such a beauty she'd replace
each loyal heart who'd plead her case
before she'd encountered greeds disgrace
when terror stole from her.

Her beauty now dried blossoms in a vase,
her broken heart cannot keep pace
with a broken doll,
a beauty they have displaced
what terror stole from her.

THE RIVER SHANNON

They say the River Shannon
brings a legacy of death
with rain-damp days, the chill of night
presents a ragged breath.

They say the River Shannon
for all its beauty, charm
will steal the health of children,
bequeathing not but harm.

They say the River Shannon
flowing through the Emerald Isle
feeds the fertile meadows
for those who live awhile.

They say the River Shannon
was blessed by St, Patrick
but lately only bringing home
the trials of Limmerick.

The say the River Shannon
fills every pub, each bar
to prove the good, the bad we Irish'
are proud of who we are.

They say the River Shannon
as good, as evil knows
all souls carried by this river
are caught up as it flows.

They say the River Shannon
takes from those who may have less.
But all who love the Shannon,
they are the Lords to bless.

WE'RE IRISH FOR A DAY

In mid-March we all hold dear
corned beef, shamrocks, frothy beer;
blessing all things Celtic, far and near-
we're Irish for a day.

We'll dance the jig, we'll dress in green,
tend to get drunk, create a scene
for all the merriment we'll glean-
we're Irish for a day.

Tenors sing the saddest songs
of emerald slopes where he belongs
bemoaning millenia of wrongs-
we're Irish for a day.

Today we'll find the rainbows end
with pots of gold our labors rend.
Each drunk we know is our best friend-
we're Irish for a day.

The pipes will wail a Gaelic tune.
Everyone will be drunk soon
to howl the coming of the moon-
we're Irish for a day.

PADDY'S ON A ROLL

He taps his foot, he slaps his leg
slurs "barkeep, bring another keg!"
He swills each amber, foamy dreg.
Paddy's on a roll!

He leans, akimbo, on the bar . . .
Proclaims how grand the Irish are!
His forlorn tunes are heard afar.
Paddy's on a roll!

He drinks his fill, he buys a round;
breathes deep, he makes a bleeting sound;
embraces each new friend he's found.
Paddy's on a roll!

He gets mad, doubles his fist.
He shouts "I'll put you on my list!"
He won't leave 'till everyone's been kissed.
Paddy's on a roll!

He drinks dark ale, his Guiness stout
endeavors to allay all doubt,
he's drunk too much.
He'll soon passout.
Paddy's on a roll!

He sings, he'll laugh, he'll lose his head.
He'll eulogize the Irish dead.
He stagger home, fall into bed.
Paddy's on a roll!

He'll laugh, he'll joke, he'll shed a tear
for all things Irish he's held dear.
St. Patrick's Day's but once a year.
Paddy's on a roll!

NO CHILD SHOULD EVER DIE

Her father wished she wasn't there
under nurses, doctors care.
He screamed at God "It isn't fair!"
No child should ever die.

He gave her life, now he must wait
for answers that may come too late.
Science warns him of her fate.
No child should ever die.

He holds her hand where needles stick.
He prays she is not truly sick.
All tubes and wires technicians prick.
No child should ever die.

He stares at her angellic face.
He swears she is in a state of grace.
What he would give to take her place . . .
no child should ever die.

DOCTOR KNOWS WHAT'S BEST

Storms wail, rains fall, sirens blare . . .
soon he'll be in doctors care.
She panics, it was just a scare.
Doctor knows what's best.

A bed of white took him away-
do what the perimedics say.
There's not to do but pray.
Doctor knows what's best.

They'll take his blood, they'll say 'hold still'
give him a shot, give hime a pill,
they'll diagnose complaints until
doctor knows what's best.

They'll bind his wounds, he'll cease to bleed.
They'll give more care than he may need.
Administrators follow greed.
Doctor's know what's best.

He'll live to breathe another day
with more bills than he can ever pay.
Cue him, make ills go away.
Doctor knows what's best.

OH, NO, THERE MUST BE FAITH

Some believe that when we pray
it is the words we think to say
that cause events to swing our way.
Oh, no, there must be faith.

Some believe that when we pray
all ills will be held at bay
when powers of God come to play.
Oh, no, there must be faith.

Some believe that when we pray,
God must do just as we say
to bless us on that very day.
Oh, no, there must be faith.

Some believe that when we pray
our troubles will all drift away
to save us from an ugly fray.
Oh, no. there must be faith.

Some believe that when we pray
we'll know a better life that way-
add offerings, the tithes we pay,
Oh, no, there must be faith.

Some believe that when we pray
if we are careful what we say,
we'll offer up what pleas we may.
Oh, no, there must be faith.

IF IRELAND WAS FREE

Oh, I wander cobbled lanes,
breathe the Shannon Rivers damp
I hear folk ballads sad refrains . . .
If Ireland was free.

Oh, I'd dream amid the heather,
stroll in oceans breeze . . .
I'd loose my souls own earthly tether
If Ireland was free.

Oh, I'd wrap my arms'round spirits,
make love to selkies on the shore,
enjoying all the magic man inherits
If Ireland was free.

Oh, I'd refuse to leave this land,
not to wander far from home,
to realize each dream so grand . . .
If Ireland was free.

Oh, I would weep but tears of joy,
traipse sand and salty sea
with favors all the saints employ
If Ireland was free.

Oh, I'd spend my pot of gold
on dreams and fantasy
I'd treasure each memory I hold
if Ireland was free.

Oh. I would know my futures past.
I'd spend my lifes coin
to pave my road home at last
If Ireland was free.

THE MISSIONARY POSITION

Young men sacrifice two years
of ultimate contrition;
follow doctrine, tow the line
of the misionary position.

At nineteen they are sent away
contrary to condition;
know as elder, no idenity-
is the missionary position.

Boys who must deny desires,
committ sins of ommision
ignore the needs of human flesh
for the missionary position.

The dictates of stern doctrine tell
sins of sexual commission-
no love of others, love of selves
is the missionary position.

If they do their Christian duty
they must pay a high tuition;
ignore, sequestor, neglect the truth
of the missionary position.

Whatever book they preach from,
there always will be friction;
chaste and pure and putrified
with the missionary position.

Teenaged boys who live the lie-
it's all pretentious diction-
God never authored any book
for the missionary position.

I HAVE NOT LOST FAITH IN GOD

I have not lost faith in God
but the precepts of a man
who plagerizes holy word
to pad his selfish plan.

I have not lost faith in God
but the vagaries of life
that lead us down a twisted path
binding us with strife.

I have not lost faith in God
but the veracity of a book
whose pages evidence a lie
when we finally take a look.

I have not lost faith in God
but all of human kind
who hide the secret of the soul
so none who search will find.

I have not lost faith in God
whose pretense now prevails;
who cast the lonely in oceans vast
where all the lost souls sail.

I AM THE ORACLE

I am the oracle.
I can sense your fear.
I feel your hesitation
as your truth comes near.

I am the oracle.
I see deep within.
I can give you solace
when you feel you're mired in sin.

I am the oracle.
I can read your mind.
I know your darkest secrets
of the most weary kind.

I am the oracle.
I can save your soul.
I can tell you what to do'
to finally be whole.

I am the oracle.
I have sang the blues.
I have been where you have been.
I have wandered in your shoes.

I am the oracle.
My vision fills the skies.
I see what you fail to see
while staring through your eyes.

I am the oracle.
I'll tell you where to go.
I'll reveal the promises
that life should always show.

I am the oracle.
I support the meek.
I will love and guide you to
the answers that you seek.

I am the oracle.
Open up your eyes!
See the truths that I reveal,
obliterate the lies.

FRANKS PRAYER

Noble gold beofre the fray
increases ten fold in the time
it takes to give away to unselfish, just pursuits
without aspect of gain lines your coffers readily
so you can give again.

For each one gift
you shall see two fall into your hand.
Be mindful of your wishes.
You receive what you demand.

A pocket must be emptied
to make room for the best,
the brightest of all blessings
when given all the rest.

A watchful eye, a wary heart
may pave your path with gold-
the coin that's held too tightly
is the hardest coin to hold.

TANAS PRAYER

Every day he wakes with her,
close to form, to face . . .
Does he know if she is happy
in her sequestered place?
A friend, a partner, yet, not quite-
she doesn't fit the mold.

She knows not being family
leaves her no thread to hold.
She's quite a jewel to his wary heart,
so sure of beating true
he takes her quite for granted
not giving her her due.

A golden girl, a golden soul
whose tender web has spun
around her love so freely spent
for a prize she should have won.

#44/2009

A first for our great nation
evident today
proving freedom and equality
will finally have its say.

A young man of intellect,
a charming man of grace
rose above his heritage
with charismatic face.

Speaking with profundity
his crisp words echo still
from the sullen, dark Potomac
to the grandeur of the hill.

Our first leader of true color,
inspite of some dissent,
rode the wave of destiny
to become our president.

UNLIKELY CONFEDERATES

We are uncommon friends,
alike as night and day.
Differing in everything
we think, we do, we say.

She is from another world
so coarse, so hard, so cold . . .
circumstances wear on her
until she looks quite old.

Her face belies her years on earth;
her dark, hard-bitten days.
Her words are not my words
just as her ways are not my ways.

I don't say I can do no wrong
or that I'm always right.
But, I honestly try to dance
my way around a fight.

I never take what is not mine.
I choose my words with care.
You cannot miss what you don't have
unless you notice it's not there.

Keep the peace in daily life,
get along with neighbors.
Do your best with what you have
earned from honest labors.

Give thanks for what God's given you
(That's why you have a voice)
Don't begrudge anothers lot,
your path is your own choice.

TO DEBBIE

She may be slight of form but she
is strong in faith, in love.
She knows a home's prepared for her
with Father up above.

Some would say she lives alone
(no husband has she yet)
He's following Heavenly fathers plan
and hasn't met her yet!

She's a friend and she's a mother
and now, a grandma, too.
She knows when you trust in Father, God,
you're blessed in all you do.

Her gifts of love are many.
She gives freely every day.
She has faith that her father
will hear what she has to say.

She is formidble in courage,
in faith and love she's just as strong.
She has no doubt her path is true.
She's walked it all along.

LIARS, THIEVES

A thief travels a crooked path
(only the liars has more curve)
When they reach their destination,
they both get what they deserve.

Society won't remove their hands
nor tear their black tongue out.
They will be diverted
until they walk a different route.

The liars tell a tale of woe,
the thief knows all too well.
They care not that the path they stay
will lead them straight to Hell.

Not Hell as punishment
of devils sent by God.
But, a Hell of their own making
where life is difficult and odd.

No one Trusts a liar.
None ought to trust a thief.
Every motive, every aspect
ia a tainted, cold belief

that everything should go their way,
that the world owes them their due.
Never trust the lying thief
anymore than they trust you.

DEAD MANS FLOAT

No matter how far you swim,
no matter how strong you are,
the tide may pull you back.

Tide, time, currents
are all at odds with life.
Plankton, algae wrap around,
dragging you down.

The water is cold.
Currents eddie about you,
each crushing you,
taking your breath, your strength.

Each stroke ahead leads to two lengths back.
Muscles tense, legs grow tired;lungs strained.
Breath comes in gasps.
Each exhalation weighs heavily.
Lungs fill, empty.

Swim one more lane,
raising the swimmers soul,
fighting the current,
the under tow,
trying to stay afloat.

MA BELLE

The phone is ringing off the wall.
It's jangling my brain.
I'd let it ring until it stops
but they'll call back again.

The noise pierces quiet nights,
a shreik in every room.
I know when I pick it up
there will be messages of doom.

I'm glad I have no cell phone.
I can take a walk
avoiding my incoming calls
when I don't want to talk.

I love caller I.D.
but some folks try to use
a private, no list number-
I don't want to hear their news.

I hear the clanging in my dreams.
I hear each pause between.
I'd gladly hang up on them
but that would seem so mean.

I have a private number
but they all get it somehow.
I guess I'm finished writing-
the phone is ringing now.

THE GOOD, THE BAD

There is a dycotomy to us,
a ying and yang,
devil versus angel.

We play both ends of the field
to our advantage.

For everything good in man,
there exists an equal bad;
from sonnets to vulgarity.

We may own a softer side,
tempered by a hard heart.
Sometimes, to stop and smell the roses,
they are crushed beneath our feet.

When we rest our heads,
all dreams are not pleasant.
Nightmares skulk into slumbering souls
causing unrest.

Reactions measured in a breath,
a heart beat as tell-tale emotions
roll to vulnerability.

FOR EVERY LOVE

For every love there should be trust
if love is to travel well.
Faith, compassion both must dwell
amid debris and dust.

For every love there is sacrifice
for progress to endure,
to survive egos when unsure,
suspecting cruel device.

For every love there is reunion,
a promise meant to last,
tempered by the fires past
when joined by loves communion.

For every love there is a strength
weathering the selfish climb,
where edicts stand the test of time
to full romantic length.

For every love there is a test
not passed by all who fell
who ended in a different Hell
mapped out before the quest.

I WAS A DARK, A LONELY SOUL

I was a dark, a lonely soul
when I was very young,
with many roads to travel,
myriad songs unsung.

I was a dark, a lonely soul
who worshiped Sylvia Plath,
ever eager to follow her
down her destructive path.

I was a dark, a lonely soul
whose pieces never fit
the center of the puzzles
where no image would commit.

I was a dark, a lonely soul
preoccupied with death,
dwelling on eternity
with every anxious breath.

I was a dark, a lonely soul
who found agony a must,
whose mere existence could survive
on utter lack of trust.

I was a dark, a lonely soul
condemned to her position,
to live alone in discontent
from her lifes condition.

I was a dark, a lonely soul
who failed to be contrite,
always up for argument,
too ready for a fight.

I was a dark, a lonely soul
whose life was such a mess,
knowing full-well her destiny
was one God forgot to bless.

I was a dark, a lonely soul
who does not know where to start
to quell the hemorage of the whole,
to mend her broken heart.

TWENTY-NINE

I worry now he's come of age
where lifes realities combine
to usher in the failures
of reaching twenty-nine.

I worry at his steady pace
to relinquish the devine,
when good and evil cross his path
when reaching twenty-nine.

I worry that the life he leads
is but a dark charade, a line;
hardly any life at all
revealed at twenty-nine.

I worry as his mother
that his life may soon define,
a man so lost in his debris
in the dust of twenty-nine.

I worry few would mourn him,
raise a glass to drink his wine,
never knowing the tragedy of life
forever twenty-nine.

BEST OF FRIENDS

For love to last a lifetime,
this lover recommends,
begin and end your married days
as the best of friends.

Never go to bed too angry
that you cannot make amends.
Rise with the sun, kiss often.
Be the best of friends.

Face problems with a partner
as trouble, trials transcend.
Stand firm in a united front
as if you were the best of friends.

Love and nurture; trust and care
that when life together ends,
the two have endured all things
forever best of friends.

MY JOURNEY

My life has been a journey
as I travel this rough road
I hope to find a partner
who will gladly share the load.

My life has been a journey
as I struggle down this path.
I have the strength to bear me up,
survive the aftermath.

My life has been a journey
as I wander twisted trails.
I will take advantage
of all good this life avails.

My life has been a journey
and as I make my climb,
I am secure in the fact that I
have gone one step at a time.

My life has been a journey
and as it nears its end,
I hope that I can truly say
I know how to be a friend.

MARRIED LIFE

When I entered married life,
I reveled in the measure
of every goal, each valued day
I would grow to treasure.

When I entered married life,
I joined a winning team,
secure in my unity
with one who shares my dream.

When I entered married life,
I vowed to share my strife,
to be partner, friend and confidant
as well as a wife.

When I entered married life,
I promised to fulfill
each vow, each promise made in trust
that I'm embracing still.

When I entered married life
I sactified our past,
a building block upon lifes road
for a journey meant to last.

INHERIT THE SON

It will be my place to carry him
now, that his mother is gone.
I see her face in his,
the mark of caring on his soul.
Her liberating love for him
set him free to be a man.
A strong heart that heals,
she gave him that,
molded by her embrace.
She loved him enough to let him go
down the road to manhood.
Letting go to gather closer-
the steadfast habit of her love.

EXECUTING WORDS

As swift as the swordsman of Calis
(and as sharp)
words reach the heart in a clear line.
Cleanly and without question as the truth
the message is deftly delivered.
No truer aim than from a champoins quiver.
Steady, skilled delivery;
nouns, verbs sharp as spike.
Feelings are such large targets
to be easily cleaved by the unkind word.

HOMES

A home is not a dwelling,
having niether doors nor walls.
Windows let in light, streaming softly,
through the halls.
Doors will always open.
All are welcomed there.
Grace and hospitality,
much friendship to spare.
Rooms, safe with comfort,
where there is love and happiness.
All who cross this threshold
are the Lords to bless.
For all who gather with us,
for those who visit here,
welcoming in graciousness
each that is held dear.
So, sit down at our table.
Have a bite or two.
All has been made ready
and we're waiting just for you.

AUTUMN REVERY

Who were they
before muscles betrayed,
gnarled digits ruled their movements?
Homecoming queens, quarterbacks,
scholars one and all . . . .
Now, so bent, all stooped;
shuffling, stacatto, along in walkers;
creeping, slouched in wheelchairs-
no cheers echo, no jumps in the hallways.
Ponytails replaced by blue boufants.
Rugged good looks now haggard, worn.
Lost in the debris of time,
all memories of straight backs, limber apendages
wait for moments of clarity,
days flying by with no promise of escape.

MOON RIVER

Caught with your pants down.
Unknowingly mooning the world,
rhetorical pants around your ankles
trip you as you try to get away.

THE HOUSE

The day they knocked the old house down,
cockroaches came scurrying out,
marching to the thrum of bulldozers.

Dol collections, photographs intermingling
with plaster, boards, shingles.

Dust rises up from the trash-strewn yard-
old tires, a stolen grocery cart, bicycle parts . . .
All the neighbors gather 'round to cheer
the demolition.

100 PROOF TEARS

He's here every night,
leaning on the bar,
shrouded in blue haze.
telling the same, tired tale.

Those who sit close,
begin to move away.
He drones on,
a catch in his voice.

The job he hates,
the girl that got away,
the son that never calls . . .

He drinks his vodka straight,
peering into his heavy glass.
He sees his future and his past
mingled with the ice.

He cries a solitary tear
that travels down his leathery cheek
to pause on quivering lips
mixing tears and Absolute.

SOPHISTICATE

Romeo
lives life on his own terms,
slender, regal
impervious to his surroundings.
Draping himself on the back of a chair,
he seems disinterested,
day-to-day occurances
according to his schedule.
He will come and go at will.
Time is his to mete out as he chooses.
Close the door, go to bed,
he'll find his way in
when it suits him.

RENEWAL

We made our vows many years ago,
for better or worse, in sickness and in health . . .
Our vows will be tested.
Things like this don't happen
to people who have worked their whole lives,
finally, to retire, to enjoy life.
The clock is ticking.
Wake up time sounds,
not by bell or buzzer
but by Cat scan, X-ray, MRI,
delivered by technicians, trusted doctors.
Brain atrophy, less elastic lungs;
dementia, lung disease . . .
Cancer? It couldn't be.
It's not the man becoming the nightmare,
but the nightmare becoming the man,
effecting all who touch him.
But, for better or worse, in sickness, in health,
we're in this together.

NOT UNTIL MADISON

It really didn't hit me,
the magnitude,'
the gravity of it all,
until Madison.
Leaving Chardon,
working all day with people familiar
to this affliction
kept my mind whirling al day long.
From the girls I work with
to my favorite residents . . .
but the weight of it, the diagnosis . . .
Alzhiemers
dementia
En-stage lung disease
until I hit Madison.
How could it be?
These things don't happen to nice guys,
to good people, to people who are in love . . .
who made a vow-for better or worse.
It didn't seem real, not until Madison.

TO BETTY

She's faced the hardest times one could imagine.
So many times, her eyes fought back the tears.
And, when any other would have crumbled,
she bore the weight of all her fears
in a fragile world made her own.
Finding her strength in faith,
in helping others who travel beside her,
offering a steady hand.
She found support by living;
she found life by accepting;
acceptance and friendship by being a friend.
Never asking more of others
than she was willing to give of herself,
she touches others by giving a tender strength,
a true friendship.

SUMMER DREAMS

The fans are on the warpath,
winning what is lost.
A million dollar contract
is all that it will cost.
A prolific bat, a seasoned glove;
a team that strives to score above;
to win a game
regardless of the wealth, the fame.
A bunt, a foul, a mighty blast;
a homerun that will echo
from baseballs mighty past.
The Mantles and the Gerhigs
are nothing but a dream,
wrapped up in a memory
of one celestial team.
Each day they practice, working out,
improving theri position.
They move ever toward their goal
of sanctified condition.
The horsehide and the leather,
the rosin bag in hand
will lead the nations favorite sport
throughout an eager land.
They only play nine innings
(unless there's overtime)
A zero-zero perfect game
borders on sublime.
The countries favorite pastime-
peanuts, dogs and beer-
accentuate the meaning
of what's been happening here.

The call goes to the bull pen,
the closer takes the mound;
wraps the game up tightly
in plays that will upstound.
The commisioners, the players
in concert as a team,
band together as a until
persuing summers dream.

WHERE DOES TIME GO?

Where does time go?
Can it be we're growing old?
Too soon we will be mouldering
beneath the sod, so cold.

Where does time go?
Have we done all we must
to realize our every dream
before they turn to dust?

Where does time go?
What battles have been won?
Will any of it matter
when this lonely life is done?

Where does the time go?
Days, moments, hours fly by-
will we be held accountable
for time wasted when we die?

Where does time go?
Has every hair turned gray?
Will our lives be recalled by anyone
as having passed this way?

Where does time go?
So many years have passed.
Our hope is to have lived life well,
enjoying to the last.

Where does time go?
Why must each life fly?
WHy are there never answers?
Why do men wonder why?

SUM OF INTOLERANCE

An act that raises hackles
as angr rears its head,
recalls the evil cackles
of those who mock the dead.

An act that raises hackles
when calm heads should prevail,
when the fire of anger crackles
as violent hands assail.

An act that raises hackles
when we should hold our tongue
bind the angry in stout shackles
after hurtful words have stung.

An act that raises hackles
when speech is void of tact,
the skill each one must tackle
is the thought before the act.

FOR

For all your efforts in this life,
what will you leave behind,
with the woman made your wife,
were you ever just or kind?

For every hour of honest work,
for every dollar made,
what spiritual value did you shirk
when you found yourself afraid?

For every son brought to this world,
born in a state of grace,
what causes of regrets were hurled
when you tried to save face?

For every wrong was there a right
to justify your acts,
when you'd fight the unjust fight
regardless of the facts?

For every heart you ever broke,
for every angry word,
of unresratined, blind anger spoke
no matter how absurd;

For every pain you suffered when
you were an innocent child,
if you forgive all, yourself and others,
your past is reconciled.

MY FAIREST CHILD

My fairest child, my daughter,
my hopes, my dreams combine
possesses no true attributes
akin to the devine.

My fairest child, my daughter
survives at any cost,
never recognizing sacrifice
regardless of the cost.

My fairest child, my daughter
is somehow reconciled
to lay before greeds altar
each gift of God. each child.

My fairest child, my daughter,
feighns truth in every word,
swearing to her innocense
when each lie is so absurd.

My fairest child, my daughter,
although I wish her well,
I fear her path is paved wi th pain
and it leads her straight to Hell.

THESE CHILDREN

These children as they're given me,
are my caches of gold;
are my gift to eternity,
a legacy to hold.

These children as they're given me,
if souls be bought and sold,
will provide entre' into Heaven
for they are of the angels fold.

These children, as they're given me,
though life winds may blow cold,
may each be guided wisely,
to question what they're told.

These children, as they're given me,
my spirits are conjoled
to bless these darling children,
and now, as I grow old,

These children, as they're given me,
may they struggle with the mold
to fulfill their reighteous destiny
as all my dreams foretold.

THE JOURNEY ON

As I traverse this path to death,
I strive with every ragged breath
to treasure, daily, the width, the breadth
of this weary road.

As I trek this woeful trail,
I pray all the saints prevail
that all sincere efforts will not fail
to bear this awesome load.

As I walk a harried pace,
I hope when I have left this place,
that I have eluded some disgrace
if my life were to implode.

As I escape my mental trap,
I let my truths fall into your lap.
Now, you jump each aching gap
astride the horse I rode.

As I arrive at Heavens gate,
I bequeathe a quest so great,
to destinies that may come too late
for stars not to explode.

I BEG THE GODS FOR SLEEP

On nights as this when I lay awake,
I reach for solace I may take
to garner dreams just for my sake,
I beg the gods for sleep.

On nights as this when I can't sleep,
I clasp the moonlights cruel gleam.
It slips through my fingers seam.
I beg the gods for sleep.

On nights as this when I cannot rest,
I offer shadows, my behest,
when I am an unwelcome guest
I beg the gods for sleep.

On nights as this when my poor soul
is beyond fatigues control,
I wish the dark to make me whole-
I beg the gods for sleep.

On nights as this when Sleep won't wait,
I wander toward illusions gate
to survive my hapless, waking fate.
I beg the gods for sleep.

On nights as this when I am remiss,
I toss, I turn my slumbers miss
I bare my breasts for Hells sharp kiss.
I beg the gods for sleep.

BENEATH THE STARING STARS

On nights when springs moon hangs cold,
upon a scene too deep to hold,
I strip my soul, naked run
beneath the staring stars.

On nights I am bereft of bliss,
I yearn for sweet Orpheus kiss,
to grant me rest on nights like this
beneath the staring stars.

On nights when dreams escape embrace,
a cold spring moon shines on my face.
Naked, then, I flee from disgarce
beneath the staring stars.

On nights when all the world's asleep,
I find myself too prone to weep.
I bare body, soul my fates to reap
beneath the staring stars.

CARRION SPIRITS

I regret these dreams I'm sent,
refusing to, this day, relent
any sins they claim I must repent
before the breaking day.

I resist the dark embrace
of sullied arms sent in the place
of those who would defer to grace
before shadows break away.

I avoid the quaking stance
of some who lean on circumstance
while leaving every turn to chance
while events will have their say.

I recall the promise made
when treaties were meant to evade
the thrust of every plan well-laid
before some plan to stay.

HOWLING IN THE NIGHT

Indigo nights, void of rest, of sleep, of dreams,
naked stars taunt my open eyes.
Free of flesh restriction I run
howling through the night.

Velvet cloaks a glaring moon
to ridicule my wakefulness
plucking slumber from unrequited souls
howling through the night.

Plush, so soft all dark controls
when eyes close to those who trust the deep,
when spirits surrender freely goes
howling through the night.

THE MURDER OF A SOUL

When the flesh is grievously taken,
when angry tongues extoll,
gifts of angels are forsaken
with the murder of a soul.

When the death of knowledge succeeds
when the negative gains control,
abusers ignore all spirits needs
with the murder of a soul.

When the avaricious muddy facts,
when vain glorious take their toll,
Spirits perish from greedy acts
with the murder of a soul.

When the mother fails her children,
when unsuccessful in her role;
the sacred, blessed are defiled
with the murder of a soul.

When society seems so reconciled
with meager alms she'll dole.
All innocense will be revealed
with the murder of a soul.

When man, when woman cherish,
when decent men parole,
all things moral perish
with the murder of a soul.

When the world has ceased evolving,
seeming static, pole-to-pole,
planets appear to stop revolving
with the murder of a soul.

RESPOSIBILITY

A child springs into this world
fresh from the hand of God-
innocent, clean, good.

It is Heavenly Fathers plan
to cherish, to be loving
as every parent should.

Each immaculate soul entrusted to our care,
to nurture, love as Gods reminds us
why He chose to place them there.

We are to hold safe, securely
each comprised of dust
sent from angelic realms elsewhere.

We welcome the child once unknown
to treasure to garner their trust, to instruct them
to release them once they are grown.

IS THIS MY LIFE

Is this my life? Is this all?
My summer answers autumns call.
Fair days of spring I can't recall.
Is this, at last, my life?

Is this my life? Is this all?
Does day survive its nightly fall?
Sun dripping through trees once tall . . .
Is this, at last, my life?

Is this my life?Is this all?
Winter howls to summers brawl
vanquished in horizontal squawl.
Is this, at last, my life?

Is this my life? Is this all?
Shadows cling to every wall.
I'm as useless as a broken doll.
Is this, at last, my life?

Is this my life? Is this all?
Humbled, now, I'm forced to crawl.
I trip, fall prostrate and I sprawl.
Is this, at last, my life?

STARLET

Sweet injenue, dear starlet,
the understudy, the star;
each prom queen becomes a harlot
unknown for who they are.

Bright injenue, sweet starlet
transported, a borrowed car.
the prom queen and the harlot
will travel just as far.

The injenue, the starlet,
each knock the door of fame.
The prom queen and the harlot
are never known by name.

The understudy and the star
are well-practiced in the game.
The injenue, the starlet
find their credits quite the same.

The prom queen and the starlet,
each a beloved daughter.
The injenues, the prom queens, too,
are consigned to gossip fodder.

The injenue, the harlot both
leave footsteps on the street
of lofty expectations
that life will never meet.

THE BELL NOW TOLLS FOR THEE

Bells toll for thee, good Christian friend
for blasphemies now at an end,
for conditions men do not recommend
The bell now tolls for thee.

Bells toll for thee, good Christian friend
for willful thoughts that never bend,
for every agony these rend.
The bell now tolls for thee.

Bells toll for the, good Christian friend
for wrongs, for hurts to never mend,
for negative acts naught to amend.
The bell now tolls for thee.

Bells toll for thee, good Christian friend
for your motivs, for an ugly trend,
for good, for evil now a blend
The bell now tolls for thee.

Bells toll for thee, good Christian friend
for evil deeds to reach an end,
for all mixed messages you send.
The bell now tolls for thee.

Bells toll for thee, good Christian friend
for self-serving favors to commend,
for proferred services you lend.
The bell now tolls for thee.

Bells toll for thee good Christian friend
for businesses you must attend,
for your soul now reaps its dividend
The bell now tolls for thee.

STAND UP AND DO WHAT'S RIGHT

If we sit back and let it happen,
if we relinquish our command,
if we decree, if we demand
we must stand up and do what's right.

If we ignore the truth before us,
if we allow another to deplore us;
if we join angry voices in a chorus
we must stand up and do what's right.

If we are complacent, do not act,
if we mistake fable for fact;
if we speak our minds, minus tact
we must stand up and do what's right.

If we refuse to see what's evident,
if we close our minds to what is meant,
if we mistake meanings of a message sent
we must stand up and do what's right.

If we turn our back on those who need
if we bow down to wealth, to greed,
if we refuse to plant loving seed,
we must stand up and do what's right.

If we take advantage of anothers lack,
if we consume yet do not give back,
if we follow, blindly, the eager pack,
we must stand up and do what's right.

If we are deaf to cries, to vows, to pleas,
If we cannot be humbled to our knees,
if we lock the doors then, hide the keys
we must stand up and do what's right.

If we are to survive the world's plight,
if we are to wake from this fitful night,
if we subtract from darkness a bit of light
we must stand up and do what's right.

IN THE GARDEN OF GOOD AND EVIL

In the garden of good and evil,
I admonish, do no harm.
We must exist in this bleak world
under auspices of charm.

In the garden of good and evil,
we must choose our path with care,
traveling down the center of
a treacherous thoroughfare.

In the garden of good and evil,
be forewarned of any wrath.
We must heed the warnings
as we travel down lifes path.

In the garden of good and evil,
all will reap what they rend
within each narrow furrow
that the gardener failed to tend.

In the garden of good and evil,
we all come face our fears,
to gather all that's planted
before the field clears.

In the garden of good and evil,
we must accept the cost
of all the deeds we rendered
or we surely will be lost.

WHEN I CLOSE MY EYES

When I close my eyes,
encourage sleep,
the voices in my head
begin dicussing attributes
of the living and the dead.

When I close my eyes
to beg for sleep,
my voices all unite
to scream complaints, their arguments
against my weary fight.

When I close my eyes,
in need of sleep,
all voices join the choir
to sing all of the praises
well rested souls require.

When I close my eyes,
I cannot sleep,
the voices in my head
rant and rave, tormenting me
offering blessed peace instead.

When I close my eyes,
encourage sleep,
the voices in my head
repeat to me, ad nauseum
"I wish that I were dead."

SEVEN MEN AND A PUSSYCAT

Seven men and a pussycat
pace about the room,
wondering which one will devine
each harbinger of doom.

Seven men and a pussycat
cannot imagine why
anyone of ill-intent
would cause a man to die.

Seven men and a pussycat
cannot count upon one hand
precepts of what's good, what's bad
while caving to demand.

Seven men and a pussycat
all hold in their breath
fearing to relax, expell
a hint of someones death.

Seven men and a pussy cat
ignore obvious fact
of any actual happenings
whe men refuse to act.

Seven men and a pussy cat
(all but one demur)
They all know the pussycats
are honest when they purr.

Seven men and a pussy cat
would never question 'why?'
all truths of men and pussy cats
are party to the lie.

Seven men and a pussy cat
can each read anothers face
knowing only one, they know not which,
will escape the lies disgrace.

Seven men and a pussy cat
pace about the room,
to wonder, save one, will eschue
their glass and concrete tomb.

Seven men and a pussy cat
caount each hour, hold their breath . . .
save pussy cats, who have nine lives.
have no need to fear death.

TO TODD, A 'THANK YOU'

You are my cherished, valued friend,
admonishing my fear,
pointing out each attribute
when my talents are not clear.

You are a treasured confidant
whose advice I hold dear
fortelling truths not always seen
when fantasy is near.

You are a man of valued trust
(unlike many-a-peer)
who can meet his image face-to-face
liking who he sees in the mirror.

THE PATH OF KINDNESS

When you walk the path of kindness
to absorb anothers lack,
giving from limited domain,
you take up the slack.
Wherever need and want decree
benevolence to succeed,
you step into the breach once more
to a position all must heed.
Where knowledge is deficient
and ignorances abound
your prayers and lamentations
for us all will still resound.
When giving and recein=ving
become equal again,
upheld in meditations
in a spiritual refrain.
When good is celebrated
and rises up in song,
blessing will be elevated
to theheights where they belong.

THE THINNING AIR

To take a breath,
to sample air;
to walk, to run
without a care.
When labored lungs
convulse to gasp
in respirations
tenacious grasp.
A deep inhale,
to take air in;
a break to breathe
to then begin
the in, the out
not so far flung
to quench, to fill
the vacant lung,
to stifle coughs
to then expire
any hint of
great desire.
the breath of life,
the urge to see;
the in, the out
will cease to be.
In equal parts
there is no doubt
if you breathe in
you must breathe out.

THE SISTER

There is a special place in Heaven
for a woman of this kind-
a better friend and confidant
would be difficult to find.
Charity and sacrifice,
self-effacing ways;
voluntary pleasures
fill her busy days.
She moves at a slower pace,
though she may seem harried, non-the-less.
Worries overwhelm her
but she is the Lords to bless.
Whatever life may bring her,
she handles it with grace.
Her deeds have shaped a destiny
that man cannot erase.
Life has dealt a heavy hand.
She's played the game awhile.
It matters not the outcome,
she will always wear a smile.

GRANDMA LOTTIE

Grandma never said a word
about anyone that wasn't good.
She taught us by example
to treat each other as we should.
When enveloped in her huge hugs,
lost in her perfumed bust,
we all knew beyond all doubt
hers was a love to trust.
Her thoughts were always with us,
even when she was away.
All she had to do was smile
to brighten up our day.
She loved everyone of us,
no matter age or size.
We were all loved eequally
in Grandma Lotties eyes.

GET A DOG

A rancid smell wafts the air;
fills the room and lingers there.
Did it come from underneath the chair?
We don't have a dog!
Something singed my poor nose hair!
It hit before I could prepare.
My nasal passages need repair.
When did we get a dog?
The aroma bodes dispair.
Has someone eaten spicy fare?
Crack a window, I don't care!
Who let in that dog?
Did flatulance create me heir
of some assy grass-fed mare?
Take her to that barn out there
then go get the dog.

THE KITCHEN SINK

All my troubles eddy 'round
to save me from the brink.
I wash my hair and all my cares
into my kitchen sink.
The steaming waters baptize me.
the shampoo saves my soul;
massages away my demons to
refresh and make me whole.
The bubbles lift my spirits
when the days have brought me down
and coax a slow, contented smile
where had been a harried frown.
The water never gets so hot
that I start to wince.
I run my fingers through my hair
continuing to rinse.
Soon I wrap my crowning glory
in a towel about my head
when I hold my tongue and temper
and just wash my hair instead.

EVELYN WAS A PARADOX

Evelyn was a paradox
throughout her checkered life.
Successful as a girlfriend, yet,
a failure as a wife.
She was the perfect mother
who was prone to some abuse.
Family never noticed and
the teachers seemed obtuse.
Known to be quite generous,
her giving knew no ends.
Her whims were unpredictable,
She was the best, the worst of friends.
She blew hot and she blew cold.
She could cook and she could sew
with more domestic talent
than she could ever show.
Evelyn was a paradox
who caused a lot of strife
when her wiley, wanton ways
ruined someones life.
She'd sell a gift you'd given her
you'd thought she'd adored.
Then, when empty handed swear
that she had been ignored.
You could never read her face.
She could lie with ease.
her family was exhausted
when they always failed to please.
It really comes to no surprise
that she could not atone.
Her victims all abandoned her.
Evelyn died alone.

FLOYD THEODORE

My dad was a burley man
who worked hard every day.
He taught me to give life my all
because that was his way.
When he was home, he tilled the soil.
You knew nature filled his soul.
Every seed he planted grew.
His harvest made him whole.
He was a wealth of knowledge
and I knew that I could trust-
I knew he'd never lie to me
and his punishments were just.
Even in his waning years
when they took his breath away.
I tried to listen carefully
to each labored word he'd say.
His ways were full of wisdom, then,
they fill my memories now.
I'd love to pass his ways along.
I wish that I knew how.

MINNIE MINNIE

Grandma was a buxom wench.
Her legs were short and bowed.
She was never still a minute-
she cooked, she cleaned, she sewed.
She had her special recipes.
There were few she shared.
I asked her for her secrets
but the others never dared.
Her apple cake was legend
and her cookies took the prize.
Everything my grandma did
was perfection in my eyes.
When she crocheted, played solitaire,
her Phillip Morris left to burn;
Minnie filled my young girls head
with all that I could learn.
My grandma was a treasure trove.
I'm glad she shared her days.
I hope I do her justice
as I emulate her ways.

GRANDPA AL

I did not know him long, you see,
but know him, yes I did.
God chose to take him away
when I was a little kid.
He taught me to drink coffee, then
with a little sugar, cream.
All these days with grandpa Al
seem just a pleasant dream.
He would sit me on his lap
when he would play his drums.
Today, music makes me think of him
when a steady rythm comes.
He played every week end night
in a local band.
We all discovered music
at our grandpas hand.
Even though his drums are quiet, now,
I hear them in my dreams again
keeping up a steady beat,
the pulse of some refrain.
His image, now, has faded some
but my memory is long.
My back slant is perfected when
I remember Grandpa's song.

IN THE DANCE

They move
together in the moment
with the music
every note a motion for surreal emotion
in the dance.
They Move
one person born of two
in each and everything they do.
they move as one,
a beating heart together
in the dance.
They move
as a unit, here, they mesmerize
an elegant serene surprise
a tale continued
in the dance.
They move
syncronizing breathless movements
Capitalizing improvements
more than partners they've created
in the dance.

THE RIGHT TIME, THE RIGHT PLACE

Serendipity-
we were meant to know each other,
to collide;
to be on lifes path
headed in the same direction.
We were positioned to meet
each others needs
at a particular time and place
in a spiritual unity of purpose.
We spend metered moments,
time allocated
to a prescribed routine
we do not follow
while being the better for it.
We are friends of some consequence,
following a schedule
in our unconventional way
until conversations lag.
We follow standard criteria,
setting aside
the confines of society
communicating at all levels-
serendipity.

MY CONSTANT MOON

In deepest shadow
on dreamless night
you are just a glance away
suspended from illusion
My constant moon.

Through summer storms
or winter howl
you illuminate my darkest side
secure in my beliefs
My constant moon.

When chill exceeds the blankets warmth,
you cover me in light
spreading illumination
My constant moon.

Throughout changes in the deep blue, in me
you remain as always known,
brilliant and illusive,
My constant moon.

TO THOSE WHO WAIT

He is a Man of some largess,
of body and of soul.
The former, not the latter,
is about to take its toll.

Life, on its course will stymie;
cease its ebb, its flow.
Brick by brick, a wall will form,
damned tributaries slow.

Breath will halt, be fleeting;
sleep be scarcly known.
Dreams, a ragged remnant,
a muffled scream, a moan.

Two steps in one direction
for one known to be still,
will take this weary traveler
to the apex of the hill.

Just one sure foot, one effort spent,
a motioning, a start;
a body prone for action,
a sum, alas, a part.

Thoughts, held back or words unspoken,
will swell, will sway,
will overflow;
the levy breached, will be broken;
no one will ever know.

KARMIC RELIEF

Put a thought in motion.
It, then, becomes an act.
Words, once they are spoken,
will then, become a fact.

A dream, upon the waking
is no less a dream
than fanciful imaginings
of another seems.

A vision to the sightless
is a vision none-the-less.
Those who know advantage
will be the last to bless.

The stooped, the lame, the sure-of-foot,
must follow the same road.
Shoulders, broad or slumping,
must carry the same load.

A hand, as it is reaching out,
will offer us much more,
something unobtainable
yet easy to ignore.

A present, wrapped with the eye in mind
can often touch the heart.
The gift, the unexpected,
sets the prize apart.

A word, a thought, a gesture;
a card, a note, a smile,
given often, given freely
lasts for quite a while.

It doesn't need a fancy box
or an elaborate bow.
It will be appreciated
more than you could know.

Be kind, be nice, be gentle;
your karma, oft repeated.
Your actions toward another soul
is how you will be treated.

MARRIAGE: TO RUTHIE

Every day, as a wife,
she blossoms, she grows;
she flourishes more
than anyone knows.

Each moment, a helpmate,
each effort made half
by the love, by the courage
to puzzle, to laugh.

A job, sometimes endless,
never seen as toil;
just another loving seed
sewn in fertile soil.

The giving, the taking;
the marriage, the match;
makes them both as equal-
that is the catch.

Not one placed so high,
not one so low
if love is encourgaed
to take root, to grow.

United, as partners,
together they go.
The road that they travel
is one they both know.

All surprises, blessings;
all changes, for the good.
Both equally contributing
what every one should.

One and one makes more than two,
two halves, more than a whole
when the union of the spirit
finds its companion soul.

RELATIVE SECURITY

A cumbersome weight bears down,
shoulders slump, weary of their burden.
Steps halting, shuffling, careful.
A kingdom to be lost, lifes work wasted
on the ungrateful, the unwilling.
A branch bowed by bending
cannot grow straight.
Blood flows, sluggish return
to the heart where quarter was given.
Young hands, uncalloused;
no sweat drips from a brow no worries furrow.
father becomes a shadow,
a bill unpaid;a duty ignored.

NATALIE

Lullabye to a wee little girl,
soon entering our world,
released from Heaven to our care.

Sent by angels to our midst–
a family's embrace,
holding safely in our heart.

Fresh eyes gaze upon faces
of love.
Gentle touch reaching deep into our lives.

Little girl, we love you,
even though you rest apart
from our waiting arms.

Your promise fills us,
expections eagerly dance
in our dreams of you.

RESTLESS NIGHTS

A sleepless night, a dream,
unknown.
No rest for the weary.

The clocks tick on,
skies open to daybreak
with tired eyes.

Deep night burns to ash
blowing away
as old bones rise.

Days brink, ready or not.

Some slow motion
catches the eye
of the well-rested.

A shuffling step, punctuated
by a yawn, blinking sight;
traveling trepidacious through the leavings of a restless night.

Books splayed, newspapers rumpled,
coffee cups ringed with residue,
making the most of restlessness.

TURN THE PAGE

Just when you think that you're as grim
as you've ever been in life,
balancing precariously on a rusty kitchen knife,
some stranger smiles
or holds a door
(or both)
Greeting you with a gleam-
suddenly your daily worries
are not what they seem.
An unexpected card arrives,
a forgotten friends 'hello'
lifts the flagging spirit up
to heights that dizzy so.
Elevated to a place
where eyes can see so far
Knowing, now, beyond all doubt
you're who you dreamed you are.
Every day has accolades.
Each day's an open book
where possibilities erase our lack
when we know where to look.

THERE SHE WAS

You thought your heart was just as full as it could get.
There would be no open space
that hadn't been filled yet.
Your love fills every inch of you.
Your soul is in full flight.
Never would there be a chance
to share that august light.
Then, there she was
wrapped in pink and smelling baby fresh.
All your heart beats moved around to mesh
with all the tender feelings
brought by Chloe'
when she came into veiw.
You realized there was plenty for her too.
There she was
dark hair and eyes so blue-
was this really possible to do?
Yet, there she was
in all her newborn glory
not just another story.
So different are the words for her . . .
your hearts music palys a different beat.
She is the long-sought puzzle piece
to make our family more complete.
Yes, there she was
a diva, a vixen as she plucks at your heart strings;
a melody, a song so fine
it's as if an angel sings.

Here she is
She sings our song.
No need to step aside.
just rearrange the corners
so everyone can see your pride.
All her love envelopes you,
you're richer now because
you needed one more jewel
to shine for you
and, there she was.

HER FATHERS HEART

She rests so comfortably
in his large, awkward hands.
He's ready.
He's prepared to meet his daughters new demands.
She needs him now,
like no other soul on earth
and so he's there for her,
the culmination of his worth.
She knows instictively before a word like 'father'
made some sense.
She knew each scent, each sound of him and hence . . .
She'll turn her head at his soft word,
greeting her with all his love
She'll never be inured.
She's safe within his secure embrace,
his sure caress.
She is his light. He is hers to bless
and bless she does.
She's the greatest gift that ever was.
She's well worth the wait, you see, because
she's beautiful, she's sweet;
she's a pip, she's a treat.
Someday, she'll grow up, she'll grow away.
Her daddys touch, his words hold sway.
His stregnth embues her with all she will need.
Imagine, beauty from a random seed.
All that she is, all that she will be
was planted from the start
to flourish, to flower, to be enjoyed
within her fathers heart.

BUBBLEGUM MUSIC

A simple melody lifting me
back to times when my young heart
was moved by music
to a place where all was possible.

Love songs, lyrics, lilting tempos
give wings to my soul
bearing me away to fantasy
where life was more attractive.

Poetry fills my days, my dreams,
reality barely garnering notice
amid bright notes,
eager words coax away the gloom.
Images, illusions holding head to pillow,
my mind wanders through fertive sleep.

Offerings from my radio
giving many options
when stolid days doled out selfishly,
all satisfying aspects of youth spent.

THE PRINCESS
(To Sara B)

Dark hair fremes her tiny face.
Deep eyes shine without.
She will grow to one of grace.
She'll erase all doubt.
Her future shines, a glowing star.
Her dreams will all hold sway.
She sees all as they truly are.
No ill will mark her day.
She knows the truth(she'll smell a lie)
No sullied lips will teach
her knowing soul,
she'll breeze them by
until bad is out of reach.
She is a wise, a knowing child.
her favor can't be bought.
All positives are reconciled.
She'll grow as she is taught.

TINAS PRAYER

A vessel of flame burns brightly.
A first quarter moon draws nigh.
Boding well of her daughters,
who keep a watchful eye.

Three circles turned in candle light
within a circle, salt.
All energies of ill will cease.
All negatives will halt.

One white candle illuminates
hels within the space,
aglow beneath the countenance
shining form and face.

Give silver to a noble cause
('twill line your path with gold)
Listen to your inner heart.
Do what you are told.

TOXIC MOODS

A bad mood is like toxic waste-
no matter how it may be contained,
it eventually seeps out,
contaminating everything.

A smile reverses s polar truth
from grimaces to frowns,
A positive light dims when pessimism
rears to anger.

Do whatever you can to keep the mood light.
Don't take life too seriously.

Remember all things are in a state of flux
poised to change in a heartbeat.

SHE RIDES

The day stretches long here before her.
Summmer advances and hides.
One friend alone understands all her cares-
she gets on her horse and she rides.

When the sun breaks on the horizon,
when beauty expands on all sides,
in the physical union of companion souls,
she gets on her horse and she rides.

Around noon they trundle the pathways,
a high sun prevails and derides,
as a team; as true partners they press on.
She gets on her horse and she rides.

As the evening approaches they tarry
in a place where their spirits reside.
Evening is done so they wait for the dawn
when she gets on her horse and she rides.

TO N.G.

My true confederate, my loving friend,
your spirit dwells with me
and binds us 'till the end.

You had an ear for all my problems.
My secrets were safe in your care.
At days end when I needed solace,
I knew you would always be there.

Your deep eyes showed every feeling.
Communicating where ever we'd be
tolerating a each small separation
no matter how long it might be.

Our long walks became our communion
We reveled in moving too fast.
You've left me with so many memories
of a friendship, a love meant to last.

BECAUSE OF HER HORSE

Whether grooming or mucking out stables
she loves every moment she spends
doing everything that she is able
for the care and comfort of friends.
Whether walking beside or astride one,
she cherishes every step
The she now lives once was only
a dream that was hers while she slept.
Her horse, every way is her savior.
Renewing her life every day.
Listening, loving and ready
to help her in every way.
In the sun, in the rain, in a snow storm,
They wander away many days
on the roads, in the fields, through the pastures
she is happy in so many ways.
No matter the work she gets into
(dirt and manure are her fate)
She will feed, she will clean, she will love them
with a love selfishess never negates.
For the grand beast she loves is quite clearly
the noblest creature of course.
She feels they deserve all the credit.
She's all that because of her horse.

FIREFLY

On deep indigo nights
fireflies fleck the low sky.
On
Off
lighting yet not illuminating.
Glittering jewels suspended
from the dark neck of a godess.
Sparkling against a backdrop of velvet.
A scattering of stars
come to earth
twinkling near the ground;
glowing for a short time
giving lustre to the mundane.

HE FELL

He fell into the bottle
where loneliness resides,
straddling a barstool
off balance side-to-side.
He fell into the bottle
Each weekend, he would drink
until alcohol and anguish
pushed him near the brink.
He fell into the bottle
The message that he sends
is punishing solitude
no sane man recommends.
He fell into the bottle
held to his trembling lips
held tightly the smooth rim
hangs from his fingertips.
He fell into the bottle
destiny demands
he find one caring person
to wrest it from his hands.
He fell into the bottle
if he has his way
he'll tumble to the bottom
where he is bound to stay.

THIRD TIME DOWN

To drown in amber liquid
to be up to ones neck
is to board sinking ship of fools
when it is bound to wreck.
Sparkling gold and foaming
reflecting every face
of fellows who fell in too far
and now writhe in disgrace.
A tall glass held within the grasp
while so cool to the touch,
leaves some men amid the ashes
of a life once loved so much.
Every day is swallowed up
in greedy little sips
Too many times a drink conceals
the lie upon his lips.
Each one follows closely-
it's one, it's two, it's three-
clouding sodden minds until
there is no other way to be.

EYES OF A CHILD

Through the unsullied eyes of a child,
vistas await, new territories surveyed.
Portals to new souls,
the eyes catch every possibility-
nothing goes unnoticed.
A life force flashes, energy effuses
from features that hide nothing.
A childs eyes capture each aspect, each idea
to the depth of life,

PRIVATE TREASURES

When I was a little girl
I had treasures I loved so.
All had intrinsic value
only I could know.
A atrnished silver ladle,
a bag of fade silk
delivered special pleasures
to collectors of my ilk.
A delicate peice of crystal,
too fargile for my touch
sat in my sacred cupboard
with china cups and such.
A tiny doll of porceline
that my grandma found
had a message just for me
when no one was around.
All of my lovely trinkets-
Only I knew of their worth-
pretty fragile items,
most precious things on earth.
i would dust and polish them,
line them up just so . . .
My heart would appreciate
what only girls could know.
These things, kept in my memory,
now gone, as all things pass,
are just as real to me today
as when they sat on shelves of glass.
The silk purse is still soft to touch.
The crystal just as fine
because it meant so much to me,
because it was all mine.

TAKE A WALK

If it's activity you despise,
there's a great new exercise.
Take a deep breath, open you eyes.
Hey, pal,
take a walk on the wild side.
If you spend your days depressed,
I have a friend who just confessed
she never liked to get undressed.
My friend,
she walks on the wild side.
If you spend your whole life taking stock,
if nobody listens when you talk,
put all your cash ibto a sock
and then, friend,
take a walk on the wild side.
If it seems your mind is in the air.
You really don't know if you care.
If you're ready to take a dare,
now, my friend,
take a walk on the wild side.
If you'll give heartstrings just a hug,
you make not need booze, nor drug.
Sublimate with just a hug.
Hey, friend,
take a walk on the wild side.

THE TEST

We roam the halls,
keep to our room.
We cultivate depression
in our tomb.
We just exist.
Our souls are numb.
We just wait until
an end will come.
We cry no more.
Our tears ran out
fromevery other question asked,
from every doubt.
We need some space
to stretch, to stand;
to have a firmer grip
within a steady han.
We must crawl out
of sorrows cave
if there is some part
of us to save.
Be patient, please,
We grow, we learn.
When it's time to choose
we takeour turn.
WE've pills and prose
to bind a thought
to the theories
psychology has wraught.
We participate.
We get some rest.
We steel our souls
for the worlds test.

We're shown the door
for days we spent
to provide a haven
now we have been sent.
We're readty, now,
the course is drawn.
it's the saner path
we now travel on.

THE ANGEL OF 5-NORTH

He speaks to those who dwell in pain,
to lift them up
to make them smile again.
He uses words, his kind rapport
to draw them out,
to make them think some more.
His comely face, his good intent
make up for all the anger
that they vent.
He gives support, offers his hand,
teaching those who balk
just how to stand.
His gentle ways,
the gentle balm
to soothe the wounded soul,
to bring it calm.
He's heaven sent.
the angels nod.
We know that surely he was
sent to us from God.

FOR RUTHIE

Her voice is a joyful carol
echoing through the halls.
Patients come out smiling
when they hear one her calls.
Her lilting tone is welcoming.
She lifts their spirits high.
Everybody cracks a grin
when Ruthie ambles by.
Her steady wit, her easy charm;
her ernest, caring ways . . .
she brightens every moment
as she works throughout the days.
her smile is contageous.
She's a champion at her game.
Now they have known her
their lives won't be the same.

PATH TO GLORY

By following a steady path
at Heavenly Fathers call,
you'll survive the aftermath
while all about you fall.
If you stray from the well-traveled road,
the people that you see
will hasten to lighten your heavy load
until you travel free.
At your Fathers constant urging,
you will come to know the way;
to know what in life needs purging
when you're kneeling down to pray.
When Heavenly Father gave you life,
by then, your lot was cast.
You'll be united for eternity
when your earthly days are passed.
Husbands, wives, the family
will gather to hear the story
after living life as meant to be
together up in glory.

SALVATION

We are not societies dregs.
We stand, now,
on sturdy legs,
standing up for ourselves.
It's true that we've
been beaten down
but our eyes can finally see
salvation come around.
It's not Allah.
It is not Jesus Christ.
The sacrifice demanded
comes at too high a price.
We can't be saved by some book
by experts on store shelves.
Our salvation comes to us
when we finally know ourselves.
It is of our very own
personal inscrutable soul-
we'ew grabbed life by the short hairs
and finally became whole.

JUST DIFFERENT

The univere is full of color-
verigated sunsets, birds of many hues;
riots of flowers fleck fields of green and gold . . .
We are not monochromatic
spectrums unobserved
by the half-open eye.
There is a perception that strange
is another word for wrong,
that change should be uncomfortable.
Different is not bad,
Difference is not wrong.
Different is just different.

ERIC'S SONG

A little boy becomes a man.
He has a dream in his soul.
He sees his words, his music
are his path to being whole.
After trying artifial ways
to reach, to touch God's face.
He found himself lost and angry
in a very heavy place.
Tears and fears;hopeless pain,
a well so dank, so deep
that all his demons captured him,
abused him in his sleeep.
One day the sun broke through to him.
He soon basked in the light;
the knowledge of his destiny
was coming into sight.
With the help of caring hands he grew.
he had help to exercise
his darker side that pulled himback
and kept him from the prize.
Now, he's whole, he's free again.
This is his life to live.
With his many gifts and blessings
he will have much to give.

A RABBIT HOWLS

I lost a little friend today . . .
a wild, little thing I'd come to love
and looked forward to seeing each day.
he would hop about the yard
where he was born;
the place where he grew up.
Today, I was outside.
th sun was a warm ball of butter
in the baby blue sky.
My pal loped about in his gray-brown glory-
ears up, whiskers twitching.
While I busied myself in the back yard,
he scampered joyfully into the field.
Suddenly, like a summer storm, an enormous hawk
careened above.
I heard it.
The heartrending howl as the raptor moved
its gigantic wings, climbing into the sky.
My little buddy struggled in the talons
of that great bird.
My soul trembled, furiously.
I wanted to do something to extrcate
him from certain doom.
The carrion monster soared ever higher
with my little friend,
Finally, the horror slid away.
Somewhere was a nest
with a hawk proudly feeding its young . . .
the cycle of life was comfronting me.

A truth . . . . nature, painfully real . . .
ultimately necessary for the survival of hawk and family.
Who is to say the more important is?
Although I will miss my little rabbit,
I will treasure the memory—
him, on the green grass, in the sun,
joyfully frollicing on my lawn.
In my memory he is eternal,
a creature of joy.

MR. PASSIVE/AGGRESSIVE

Change can chafe the steadfast man
used to the status quo;
If redirected from his narrow path,
he won't know where to go.
An altered set of circumstance,
a fast or varied pace,
brings a look of consternation
quickly to his face.
he may dain
to acquiesce
if powers so decree.
In his mind
he would endure
forever to think free.

HAPPY GRADUATION DAY

There you are.
You've made us proud.
Even in your cap and gown
you stand out from the crowd.
Our little girl,
all grown up,
ready for the world.
There you stand
before them all;
so lovely, so perfect;so wonderful, tall.
A girl of charm,
of love, of grace
who's gone ahead
to find her place.
take the lead, babe,
join the dance.
Don't be afraid to take a chance.
Be yourself
with a smile on your face.
Play the game. Win the race.

SUNRISE

This is your sunrise.
the dawn of days ahead.
A new life on the horizon
beckons promise.
Look to the sky.
The sun shines for you,
a spot light, beaming.
Your audience awaits your curtsil.
Take your bow.
Destiny applaudes,
an ovation from the sky.
Look toward your future.
Embrace what's passed.
Let the world spin,
but, hold on.
It's the morning.
There's a huge blank slate.
Fill in the spaces with your dreams.

We are only in bondage if we
allow ourselves to be...
our minds, our souls are
forever free... keep the
spirit flying ...!
                your friend
                Meryl Taylor
                2013

Edwards Brothers Malloy
Thorofare, NJ USA
July 3, 2013